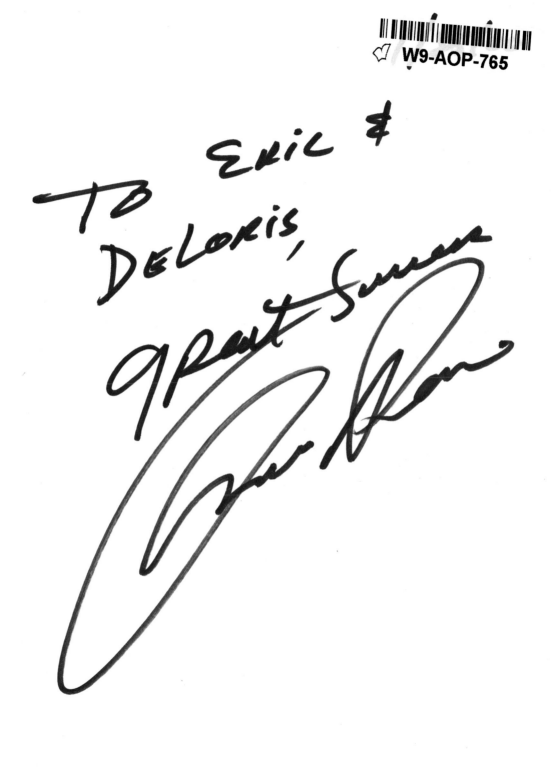

INVESTIGATIVE SELLING

How to Master the Art, Science, and Skills of Professional Selling

by

Omar Periu

Investigative Selling

Published by

Omar Periu International, Inc.

P.O. Box 812470

Boca Raton, FL   33481

Library of Congress Catalog Card No.: 75/275,530

ISBN: 1-893444-00-07

Printed in the United States of America

First Edition

For sales inquiries and special prices for bulk quantities, please contact Omar Periu International, Inc. at 800-789-3232 or fax to 561-479-2282 or write to the address in the back of this book.

ABOUT THE AUTHOR

Although the terms "dynamic," "high-energy," and "super achiever" all describe Omar Periu as he is today, they aren't exactly the words which portrayed the results accomplished in his early sales career. Initially, Omar had little understanding or success with the sales process and its outcome. However, after studying the masters, and observing the difference between the performance of top salespeople compared to those barely squeaking by a living, Omar developed *The Investigative Selling Principles*. With their implementation in his own sales career, it wasn't long before Omar became one of the top professionals in his field.

His tremendous success led him into sales management, and before the age of 31, Omar was a self-made millionaire, owning some of the most profitable health clubs and sports medicine facilities in the United States. From his modest beginnings as a take-it-on-the-chin salesperson, Omar knew the pain of sales rejection and failure. He also discovered the high of mastering sales presentations and sophisticated closing skills, and, most importantly, he is now teaching these unique investigative principles to salespeople, managers and entrepreneurs all over the world. Like Omar's experience, having internalized these principles, his students are now reporting their greatest sales triumphs ever.

The contents of this book are fresh and inspiring, and his story is unforgettable. Now a world-traveled speaker, who has spent nearly a decade educating salespeople worldwide, Omar has personally delivered more than 2,000 seminars, workshops and training programs. He has trained over one million people in more than two-thirds of the Fortune 500 companies. He has been a featured speaker at events with superstars Zig Ziglar, Tom Hopkins, Brian Tracy, Harvey Mackay, Og Mandino, Jim Rohn, Terry Bradshaw and Lou Holtz, among others. He is a member of the National Speakers Association and has been inducted into the prestigious International Platform Association. Now, he is author of his exciting new book *Investigative Selling*.

Through hard work and determination, Omar became recognized as a highly professional salesperson, and you can do the same. He is committed to helping people like you achieve their full potential through mastering *The Investigative Selling Principles* presented in this book. To quote Omar's philosophy: *"Success is in the moment—so make each moment count!"—Omar Periu*

DEDICATION

I dedicate this book to my parents, Oduardo and Nelida Periu, whose faith, love and belief in me gave me the purpose, strength and perseverance to never give up, no matter what.

ACKNOWLEDGEMENTS

It has been a dream of mine to write a book that would help sales professionals to achieve great success. The goal is now a reality. However, it wouldn't have been possible without the help of many important people in my life. The first I would like to thank is my wife, Helen. Her encouragement, patience and love have kept me focused on this important goal. Thank you for believing in me.

I would especially like to thank my mentor, Tom Murphy, who over the years taught me how to be a true sales professional and gave me the wisdom to realize what success in life really means. His concepts, insights and suggestions have truly made this book a new standard in sales training. "Murph," as I affectionately refer to him, continues to be a real inspiration. Thank you Murph; I will always be grateful to you for changing my life.

My special thanks go to Tom Hopkins, the legendary sales trainer of our times. It was through his mentoring that I learned how to be a great trainer. Thank you, Tom, for your support and friendship.

I'd also like to thank Debi Siegel, whose untiring efforts of research, writing and development, putting my words on paper, made this book possible. Her efforts were outstanding. Also, a special thanks to Judy Slack for revising and fine-tuning the contents of this book. Her talents contributed immensely to its professionalism.

Most of all, I'd like to express my appreciation to you, the reader, for believing in me enough to read this book. You will become amazingly successful if you'll learn and implement this material. You have the ability, so never give up, no matter what!

WHAT YOU'LL LOSE IF YOU DON'T OWN THIS BOOK

Not a day passes that you couldn't use the effective strategies, proven techniques, creative methods and common sense presented between these pages Whether it's to promote or persuade, to convince or consult, the implementation of these principles will bring you greater success and satisfaction in both your personal life and sales career. Applying the principles you will learn after reading this book will help you to attain financial freedom, enjoy a renewed energy and enthusiasm for your work and graduate to a new level of professionalism. The fact is, you simply cannot afford to miss this opportunity!

Take a look at where you stand in your sales career, NOW! Could your customer relationships be improved? I have experienced that and given you solid tools to build the foundations of great customer relations! Could your questioning techniques and presentations be more customer-focused? I was once unable to direct and manage the selling sequence because of poor selling skills, however, now I can offer practical, hands-on methods of discovery and demonstration that lead you to a successful close! Could you be more creative with your prospecting endeavors and more thorough in your follow-up? I went from fear to fulfillment when it came to prospecting and follow-up, and the principles introduced in this book will enable you to do the same. The thing to remember is this: if positive change is what you seek—it cannot be achieved through the same old negative behavior. Knowing this, can you afford to miss this opportunity?

How many more times can you say to your family—"We can't afford that"—before you feel beaten down and disadvantaged? What else will you try to improve your sales performance, before telling yourself—"I'm just not cut out for selling"—and giving up what could have been the perfect career for you? Who will you have to turn to when the market's down, the prices are up and you're stuck in mediocrity? Myself and all the other professionals in this book who have offered their experiences as examples and knowledge as counsel—that's who you will have to turn to! This opportunity, you absolutely cannot afford to miss!

If you are saying to yourself . . .
- I need to feel financially secure.
- I need to set and achieve greater sales goals.
- I need to have more freedom to enjoy my family and friends.
- I need to better serve my customers.
- I need to create my own success!

The proven techniques in this "how to" book will increase your income, immediately. However, first you need to take your sales career seriously by taking this book home with you, tonight.

FOREWORD

It has been a highlight in my life to see a living example of everything I teach. Over the years, many of my students have mastered and succeeded with my how-to selling skills material. Few have ever taken it to the level that Omar Periu has. He not only succeeded as a salesperson, he truly internalized and customized our training to his particular industry. He then began doing what Champions do—helping others to succeed—always giving credit where credit was due. His movement into sales management and training has been and will continue to be a benefit to students of selling practices today and in the future. I have never seen anyone work harder on self-development and self-improvement than Omar. His goal to provide you, the reader, with quality training and the motivation to succeed is sincere. His wisdom in developing the material you're about to read is profound. Questioning is the foundation of all professional selling. The development of *Investigative Selling* is an excellent approach to helping salespeople understand and learn strategies and tactics that practice has proven to be sound.

Omar Periu exemplifies the work ethic, discipline and commitment of a true Champion salesperson, sales manager and trainer. I will forever be indebted to him for his commitment to helping me spread the message of professionalism in the fields of sales and management. Read the book. Practice the strategies. Then, reap the rewards!

Tom Hopkins

Helpful Icons

Throughout this book, I have placed easy to identify icons that indicate important points that needed to be emphasized. Their explanations are as follows:

 Closing the sale; or, your commitment to success.

 A reminder. Either the topic was talked about in a previous section of the book, or it is introducing a skill that you need to remember to use.

 Represents something that you need to stop doing, immediately. This is usually something that can kill the sale.

 These are tips and skills that, if applied properly, will substantially increase your income.

 Listen carefully; this is a clue to great personal and professional success.

Helpful Icons (cont.)

    Important points and ideas that need to be noted.

    Key points in the text that, when implemented, promise great results.

    These are suggestions that you may want to try in order to improve your performance.

    Things you can do to get into the character of an investigative salesperson.

    Very important points that have been magnified for your investigative sales success. These are the specific points that differentiate you from the average salesperson.

Contents

INTRODUCTION
My Inspiration for Investigative Selling

For over 20 years, I have been fighting a battle with the salespeople I've been training in my businesses. As I now conduct training for companies all around the world, I continue to fight the same battle with potentially good salespeople just like you. The battle is in helping each salesperson to reach his or her peak performance, day after day, week after week, month after month, year after year. That's when selling becomes fun; when you are **consistently** outperforming your own expectations. Don't we all want to do more of what we do best? The better your sales performance, the more you'll sell. The more you sell, the more success and happiness you will experience.

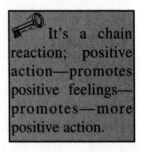 It's a chain reaction; positive action—promotes positive feelings—promotes—more positive action.

In the beginning of my sales and management days, not only was I experiencing a battle over how to teach selling skills that bring about consistently positive actions, but the battle was quickly escalating into a full-fledged war as well. The need to improve selling skills was the battle; the war was much more difficult to identify and win. It was a war in the salesperson's own mind. Because my salespeople shared with me their frustrations in establishing ongoing, **consistent** success, I decided it was time to evaluate the source of their frustration and find a teachable solution. That's exactly what I'm going to share with you in this book, how I won the battle and you can too!

Consistency Was Critical

I needed to create a fresh strategy, to form a mold that salespeople could fit themselves into, and in doing so experience immediate and consistent success in sales. I got to thinking about the salespeople who were thought of as "naturals". They all had certain characteristics that gave them consistent, positive end-results. Characteristic?

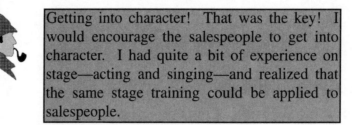

Getting into character! That was the key! I would encourage the salespeople to get into character. I had quite a bit of experience on stage—acting and singing—and realized that the same stage training could be applied to salespeople.

That's exactly how *Investigative Selling* was born—right out of the needs of the salespeople I train!

When I discovered how well the *Investigative Selling Principles* worked, that's when I decided to write a book on the subject and make teaching those principles my number one goal. What would I accomplish? I'd win the war! I'd help salespeople to **consistently** act and feel like the professionals I knew they could become.

First things first, though. I had to discover what created the inconsistencies. I began to ask questions, listen, observe and take notes in order to solve the problem of what made some salespeople outstanding performers while others appeared to work just as hard and get nowhere. Every day for five and a half years I would ask myself the question: "What did superstar salespeople do, or not do, that separated them from those who were average performers?" My research continued, and for two decades I have observed the industry greats and listened to their messages. I have attended hundreds of seminars and watched and listened to every audio/video tape I could find on sales. I have read hundreds of books and recorded every detailed technique, no matter how seemingly insignificant, in order to discover the specific sales methods and strategies that separated the exceptional from the average.

I was focused on a mission—a mission to gather information on every aspect of sales and find solutions for every type of selling situation. As I gathered the information to write this book, it became apparent to me that I was also practicing the exact skills necessary to become a highly successful salesperson. **I was asking questions, listening, observing, taking notes, problem solving, discovering new closes and practicing effective follow up.** I was acting as an investigator! I also came to the realization that adopting this style is what I had been doing all along in my selling career and it worked.

One of the most important keys to successful selling that I discovered was that almost all salespeople had a natural tendency to tell, not ask. Sound familiar?

If this sounds like you, you're keeping company with many other salespeople who have leveled off in their production and feel forever stuck in mediocrity. The challenge when you're telling is that you are not discovering all the things that can most benefit your customers.

 Telling when you should be **asking** is one of the easiest habits to fall into and the most difficult to break.

 In this book you will learn a method of control or, as I prefer to call it, a method of mastery. This mastery is not new in theory but is, for many salespeople, very new in practice. The theory is called self-mastery. Sure, average salespeople usually understand that they need to learn about their profession, but in that learning process the two most important things commonly overlooked are:

1. Mastering the fundamentals of sales
2. Understanding the need for mastering yourself

You may be asking "What do you mean by that, Omar—that we will manage the sale by first managing ourselves?" Exactly!

Doesn't mastery mean the same as control? There is a world of difference between mastery and control. The average salesperson will attempt to establish control and self-importance through nonstop talking. That is the kiss of death in sales. The first thing you must learn to do is master your own actions.

Don't Forget

Choose to be as good a listener as you are a talker. Master your selling situations by mastering yourself. Make up your mind in the very beginning to do much more asking than telling!

During my sales seminars, I found myself spending the majority of my time trying to get salespeople to limit their talking; and, train them to ask insightful questions and gather important information, instead. It was my goal to convince salespeople to focus most of their attention on being active listeners. Although salespeople heard my message and practiced these skills for a while, the natural pattern seemed to slowly fall back into talking rather than listening. They did master their actions; unfortunately, their habitual actions were the ticket for a quick exit in selling, and an income far below what salespeople are capable of attaining.

By learning better selling skills, by thinking and acting like an investigator, my own personal production and the performance of those I was training grew to limitless proportions.   Not only did the performance levels of my people continually go up, but they were also able to sustain their best sales performance peaks.

This is what investigative selling does for you. It allows you to maintain consistently high levels of production. No more peaks and valleys in sales, or better yet, no more burned out feelings of total failure. That is my purpose for writing this book, to teach you to set aside your natural tendency to **tell** instead of **ask**. In the process, you'll become a superstar salesperson all the time, not just during one or two high points every sales quarter.

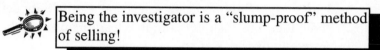

Being the investigator is a "slump-proof" method of selling!

Assuming a character is not a new concept. It's something we've all know how to do since childhood. Do you remember playing "pretend" games when you were a child? Everyone has at one time or another. You may have taken on the characters of your favorite television hero or a sports figure. Perhaps you even pretended being another member of your family. Girls often pretend being "mommy," while boys pretend filling in their dad's shoes. When we grow up, many of us forget how much fun it was portraying someone else. Some of us, however, continue the magic through theater or singing opportunities and it can prove to be a great advantage.

When I was young, I trained to be a professional opera singer. In the opera, singing and acting requires much more from you than just learning lines and staying on key. To deeply move the audience, you have to really get into the song and live the part until you become the person in that particular piece of music. It is no longer a pretense but, instead, you are in a changed state. You have taken on new traits, feelings, and actions in this new state. To make your part come to life for your audience, you must become the part. True top performers draw on all their own experiences, causing them to feel and act the same way as the characters they portray.

Believe it or not, you can apply the same principles to becoming an outstanding salesperson. How?

Get into character. Just like the great singers, actors and actresses who move their audiences, you can get into the character of a great investigative salesperson and move your customers to own your product and service.

The role of investigator is really very simple to assume. Think about it; you've grown up watching this role played by dozens of people who all adopt the same characteristics. They all ask questions. They all search for facts and information and, in the end, with a lot of hard work and determination, they solve the case.

What I have learned, and what I teach, is the importance of becoming a warm and friendly fact-gathering professional who listens to answers and takes notes. I have learned the value of being a salesperson who leaves no stone unturned to discover any clue that will help the customer. How did I do this? I got into character and became the investigative salesperson. I asked questions! I soon discovered the only way I could learn while I was talking was if my words were in the form of a question.

The following story illustrates how my sales career skyrocketed to a level I'd only dreamed of achieving, simply by becoming an investigator. Here is the story of my experiences and how some of those experiences influenced my selling career.

Early in life, I felt all the odds were against me. I was born in Cuba, but was brought to the United States at the age of seven. It was 1961, and communism in Cuba was closing in on successful businessmen like my father who prospered by doing business with American-owned companies. My father knew that Castro's propaganda about the evil Americans was not only a lie, but would also end up crippling the Cuban economy and the spirit of its people. There was nothing left for my father to do but plan his family's escape to America.

Although I remember very little about our secret flight to Miami, I do recall the fear in my mother's eyes as we left my father behind, telling our neighbors we were taking a short visit to friends. We couldn't take the chance to leave as a family for fear we would be detained and Castro would discover our plan. Communism not only destroyed our financial security, but also threatened to take my father's life. Circumstances had dealt my parents a terrible blow, but they chose to turn their loss into one of life's great lessons for themselves and their children.

My parent's journey was a long one to freedom, and it was then that I learned one of the most important lessons in my life. Free enterprise is rarely free! It had cost my father his business and successful career, my mother her home, and all of us our friends and family.

As it turned out, I was very blessed! My father did not give up! Instead he got out of Cuba, following us to Miami several weeks later. We were poor, but safely deposited on American soil. To this day, I thank God for St. Patrick's Church, which sponsored our family and welcomed us to the United States. It was a stressful time for all of us and those early years in America were tough on everyone, but I always felt protected by the love of my mother and father and their reassurance that we would find happiness.

Going to school in a country where you can't speak the language came with its own set of special opportunities. To most of my schoolmates, I appeared to have nothing. My father taught me otherwise. He taught me to be a winner! The more he reinforced my ability to achieve, the more I did just that. When I wanted to win the 100 yard dash or become the number one weight lifter in my school, my father told me stories of the long line of men in our family who were the fastest and the strongest in all of Cuba. He gave me a precious gift—an unwavering belief in my abilities to succeed, no matter what. He instilled in me the true spirit of a super salesperson.

 I hope to achieve with you what my father did with me; creating that "I will succeed" belief in yourself that refuses to be compromised by hardships and temporary failures. I didn't even recognize the importance of what my father was teaching me back then, so distracted was I by rejection, failure and countless disappointments.

I am no smarter than you, but I have learned to use my skills and take massive action in order to get the best return on my time and efforts.

> If you have great personal difficulties that sometimes get in the way of your success, you have two choices:
> 1. You can choose to let them burden you and inhibit your performance
> 2. You can choose to rise above the occasion and follow your dreams.

Do you give up or get up? I chose, like my father before me, to get up, but I must admit to a stumble or two before getting my bearings.

One stumbling point was when I was nineteen years old; I felt my future slipping away.   Suddenly all my plans had gone awry. I was studying voice performance at Southern Illinois University. Half way into my third year, my father suffered a serious heart attack. There was no question about it, I was flying home to be by his side and offer him the love and encouragement he desperately needed. Having been away from school for a few weeks, my return was less than the welcoming home of the prodigal son. Professors had already administered and graded finals, and they were none too excited about the prospect of make-up examinations. I was just another kid who had his whole life ahead of him. What was a six-month delay going to hurt?

To them it was nothing; to me it was a lifetime. I wasn't about to lose that time so, instead, I'd show them. I quit school! Looking back I realize it was a big mistake on my part. I've always regretted not staying in school and getting my degree. I guess there are few people who could say they have lived their lives with no regrets. One thing I've done, however, is learn from that mistake, and help others do the same by speaking to students around the country on the importance of staying in school. Instead of dwelling on the negatives, I choose to move forward and be productive. In sales we must practice that same principle.

 Dwelling on the negatives only makes those negatives stronger, but learning from them makes the experience a worthwhile one that will bring about future successes for yourself and others around you!

Dropping out of college solved nothing; it only served to make me depressed, desperate for money, and incredibly angry! Forget it, I thought! I would save some money and go to California and make it as a top recording artist. However, in order to save money, you have to make money. So, I lived in my brother's basement in Joliet, Illinois and found a job as a laborer in a stone quarry.

I don't know if you are familiar with what working in a stone quarry is like, but let me give you a little picture of my own corner of hell. It's ten hours a day working approximately thirty feet under the ground, wearing a complete hearing and breathing apparatus and decked out in a hard hat and padded clothing to protect you from the flying stones. For me it meant swallowing more stone dust than solid food. Day in and day out it was my job to repeatedly clean and grease the pulleys that were caked with the residue of finely crushed stones. I came home every day with a broken back and, even worse, a broken spirit. It was a hopeless, thankless job and that is exactly how I felt. Have you ever had a job that you hated so much it brought tears to your eyes? If so, you'll know exactly how I felt. Angry! I hated my job. I hated my life!

After almost a year, I saved up enough money to pack my GTO with a U-Haul carrier on top of my car, and off I went to California. The thing about life is that events happen that you least expect, and so went my trip to stardom. A heavy wind blew the U-Haul carrier off the top of my car and all was lost. When I arrived in California, I paid for the damaged carrier and had just enough left to rent a tiny studio apartment. My voice had taken a beating working in the stone quarry, and my pocketbook was just about as empty as my dream of becoming a singer. Being resilient, I turned to the one thing I knew better than most: weight lifting and training.

Since I had broken almost all the records in lifting, from high school through college, and knew how to build up the body through proper nutrition and exercise, I got a job working as a trainer in a health club. Now I could have some luxuries in life, like food on the table and a roof over my head. Being a personal trainer was natural for me, but I needed something more.

Believe it or not, that need for more is the emotional rocket that acts as the catalyst for many extremely successful salespeople. What other career besides sales can offer you financial freedom and limitless opportunities to succeed?

That is exactly what I saw. All around me, salespeople for the company were able to make a lot more money selling, so I decided to give sales a try. That "give it a try" attitude was my first mistake. I don't need to tell you that nobody ever made it big in selling with the attitude that they would give it a shot, right? It wasn't much different for me. I wasn't exactly setting the world on fire with my $147 dollar monthly income for my first 9 months in sales.

About the only thing I *was* able to set on fire was the carburetor of my ten year old GTO. In fact, my friends used to tease me that it smoked more than the burning city of Atlanta in *Gone With the Wind*. I didn't have to worry about what my dates looked like; I couldn't see them anyway for all the smoke and fumes. My car smoked so much oil I couldn't see the light change at the intersection, and revving my engine put the entire neighborhood in danger of respiratory attack. By all outward appearances, I was far from being special.

The other thing I couldn't see was how I would ever be able to make a go of selling. Instead of thinking about improving my skills and increasing my income, I was too busy feeling sorry for myself and being angry. Was success meant for everybody but me? Here I was, personal trainer to the stars, surrounded by highly successful people, and I was getting angrier by the day. There just had to be a way to get more out of life! Pardon my intrusion in the story, but many salespeople look at top producers and ask themselves the same question: "Is success meant for everybody but me?" Let me take a moment to assure you that you are on the road to success right now as you are reading this book. It is meant for you. It's definitely meant for you!

However, I didn't quite believe this concept, yet. One day's worry ran right into the next until the discouragement and depression were driving me further and further from a desire to sell. Even more importantly, I began to doubt my belief in myself. Since I was a young boy my father had taught me to love America, to believe in my ability to become anything I chose. I knew he wouldn't have lied to me all those years. Why would he have brought me from Cuba to America, the land of opportunity, if I didn't have as good a chance as everybody else to become a great success? Without even realizing the importance and impact of what I was doing, I began to question my situation and myself.

Late one afternoon I was sitting at my desk at the health club where I worked, gazing out the window. Many of you would probably recognize the activity. It's what many unskilled salespeople call "prospecting" (yeah, right). I had, once again, failed to close a membership sale and my thoughts were of an empty wallet and an empty future.

Suddenly, my attention was taken by a larger-than-life, black 6.9 Mercedes that pulled up outside our doors. I had never seen a car like that before, and being a mechanic's son, its smooth lines and powerful sound intrigued me. But what intrigued me even more was the handsome, well-built man who stepped from behind the wheel. He wore the clothes and jewelry of a powerful man. He just reeked of success. He walked with direction. He knew where he was going and how he would get there. "Wow," I said to myself. "If I could be just like him!" Have you ever seen a man or woman with that kind of presence? Right then I knew what I wanted. I wanted the same success, the same self-confidence, the same respect he had.

He walked inside, met with the owner, and then left before we had a chance to meet, but I was determined to discover more about him. That evening I talked to David, the club owner, and asked: "Who was that man who came in to talk with you today?" I was right. He was as successful as he looked: part owner in the health club and a multimillionaire, and his business was sales. I then asked one of the most important questions of my career. "David, would you introduce us?" I got my wish even sooner than I had planned, as the owner of the powerful Mercedes would be returning the very next day.

"Omar Periu, I would like you to meet my friend and partner, Tom Murphy." There was no more buildup; David left the rest to me.

"Mr. Murphy, I'm happy to meet you," I said, as I offered my hand. Then I did something my mom and dad had told me. "Would you mind if I asked you some questions over lunch or coffee today?" I asked. I sensed he could tell I was hungry for success.

> If you want to learn from successful people, ask them to lunch or out for a cup of coffee and then question them about their success.

"Certainly Omar," Tom said. As we had lunch, Tom asked, "What do you do at the health club?"

"I'm in sales," I said.

"What's your average income?" he asked.

"About $147 a month," I whispered, expecting him to begin a heavy conversation of everything I should be doing to become a success just like him.

Instead I heard him say with an undercurrent of humor, "Well, there's room for improvement!"

For the first time in weeks I was able to laugh at myself; a very important thing to do in sales—keep your sense of humor.

> Highly successful salespeople can laugh at their mistakes. They recognize that everybody makes them, but the difference between learning from your mistakes and letting them kill your career might be in the ability to laugh at yourself. Laughter is a great medicine!

He advised me to see a man named Tom Hopkins, the nation's number one sales trainer, and it just so happened Mr. Murphy was CEO of the company. It sounds very impractical now, but I invested my last $155 to pay for a seminar in town being offered by their company, and Tom Murphy kept his promise to give me books and tapes for free, called *How To Master the Art of Selling.* The rest is history, but it certainly wasn't a story of overnight success. Murph became a great mentor in my sales career and a close and respected friend, introducing me to other greats like Zig Ziglar, Earl Nightingale, Dr. Maxwell Maltz, Og Mandino, Dr. Norman Vincent Peale, Dick Gardner, and many others willing to share their successes.

Time passed and our relationship matured. I shared with Tom Murphy my desires of becoming a professional singer and how I thought selling could get me there if I could ever get the hang of it. At first Murph laughed when I told him how much I thought salespeople were like those investigators I saw on television. I told him that because of my opera training, I was able to pretend. I was able to become the investigative salesperson. The more we talked, the more we kicked around the idea that there were a lot of common practices between great investigators and great salespeople.

More lunches, more workouts, more meetings of shared ideas, and Tom Murphy and I began to envision this whole investigative selling process. Tom encouraged me to develop the investigative comparison, and soon I knew that was the key to success, and my increased sales performance was evidence of that fact. Murph was actually the consummate investigative salesperson, and he helped me to identify and develop the principles in this book. Not only did they make me a top salesperson in the sports medicine, health and fitness industry, but they also moved me into the arena of international speaking. Both Tom and I have certainly seen the overwhelmingly positive results of utilizing and teaching the *Principles of Investigative Selling*. I'm more than convinced that you can experience those same positive results as well.

As our friendship grew, and my skills as an investigator improved, so did my sales performance. I went from a $147 dollar a month salesperson to the top salesperson in my industry, but I didn't stop there. Next I moved up to the position of general manager of 18 health clubs, still practicing the same proven principles with my salespeople that had consistently worked for me. That's right! I trained the salespeople in our health facilities to use the *Principles of Investigative Selling*, and soon decided to purchase a health club and sports medicine facility of my own.

> I not only discovered how taking on the character of an investigator could help my sales performance, but I also found all those skills could be **duplicated**.   Other salespeople could find the same success by practicing the same principles.

Salespeople who worked for me began to enjoy increased sales as well. By teaching them to stay in character, to ask questions and gather information, they were prospering right along with my health clubs. The first club I owned was approximately 7,800 square feet and had a membership of well over 10,000 people. Within six months my investigating selling principles increased our sales volume by 400 percent, and I was on my way to owning nine of the most successful health club and sports medicine facilities in the United States.

It soon became apparent to me that my clubs weren't experiencing the large employee turnover rates of other health clubs. Why? My salespeople weren't on that burnout, roller-coaster ride of sales, loving it on the way up and hating it all the way down. Instead they were learning. The more they learned the more their incomes grew. By developing investigative skills:

- Salespeople's success was no longer dependent on market trends or on a fluctuating economy.
- Salespeople no longer experienced the peaks and valleys of the industry.

By being investigators, we were all experiencing consistently increasing sales volumes and developing long-lasting relationships with our customers.

Within the first year, we attracted some salespeople in the business who wanted to join our team of winners. The more evolved and developed my *Investigative Selling Principles*, and the more I shared them with my sales force, the more everybody benefited. My inner questions continued. If I could teach my own salespeople how to become that successful, why couldn't any salesperson in any field benefit from the same knowledge? That became my priority—to discover whether the *Principles of Investigative Selling* could be duplicated in other areas of sales.

In 1988, I sold my health clubs and sports medicine facilities and began my dream of teaching and mentoring others to achieve their dreams. I can honestly say it hasn't been for the money, but rather for the personal rewards of seeing and hearing about the countless successes of sincere students who have attended the seminars I have taught throughout the world in English and Spanish. It all started and it continues because I'm able to stay in the character of an investigator, asking questions of all those I meet.

Salespeople who left my seminars began to feel as I did, that there was nothing better than a career in sales. When owners saw the difference in their salespeople turned investigators, they actually began offering to PAY me to develop ongoing teaching programs specifically for them. I thought, "Hey, here I am back on stage, only instead of me giving an inspiring performance, I'm being inspired by all those putting the investigative principles to work and sharing their stories with me.

Well, that's some of how I got here, but before you begin embarking on your own investigative sales adventure, I'd like to take a moment to thank those who have meant so much to me in my career. I can't tell you the benefits of being associated with Tom Murphy and Tom Hopkins. Their knowledge and experience has contributed so much to my success. I benefited from Tom Murphy's knowledge as mastermind behind the marketing, promotion, writing, speaking, teaching and training programs of Tom Hopkins International, Inc., and from Tom Hopkins' skills as an outstanding stage presence and exceptional presenter. My years of experience with Tom Hopkins International allowed me the opportunity to master the delivery of my message. I feel very fortunate to have been a part of their team, experiencing the wonders of speaking to organizations from coast to coast, continent to continent.

Now, it's time for you and I to get started on your training. Let's get into character and start investigating!

INVESIGATIVE PRINCIPLE #1
Become an Investigator—Ask Questions

CLUE:

The number one trait of excellent investigators is their ability to gather information. An effective investigator cannot gather that information without first asking questions.

"One of the best ways to learn while you speak is to formulate your words into insightful questions."

Omar Periu

Any good investigative salesperson knows that the best way to serve customers is to discover all their wants and needs, then determine how to serve those needs. This can only be accomplished by being interested enough to ask questions and then actually listen to their answers.

Although this sounds like a simple process, most sales are lost through poor information-gathering and inadequate listening skills.

> **You cannot bring a sale to a successful close and have happy, satisfied customers on a regular basis with poor fact-finding skills and weak listening habits.**

You'll be a burned out salesperson if you tell instead of ask. Doing this will bring you no greater acclaim than mere average performance. As an average salesperson, you'll only achieve mediocrity in your organization, instead of enjoying all the benefits of the most rewarding career in the world: sales. If you have been selling without the joys and rewards this wonderful career can provide, chances are, you're out of character. You're not practicing *Investigative Selling*.

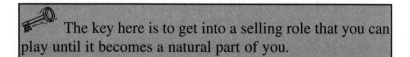

> The key here is to get into a selling role that you can play until it becomes a natural part of you.

The reason this works is that you now have a role to model yourself after, a standard of behavior that has worked extremely well for me and others in this profession, and it will work the same or even better for you. It's a pictured method of behavior that is simple and easy to **duplicate**.

When we are new in selling, we don't know how to act and, as I said before, talking seems to be much more natural than asking questions and actually listening to your customer. By getting and staying in character as an investigator, your results will be much more consistent. You know that by playing the role of investigator you will always help customers get the total solution they want by evaluating the facts and clues they have given you.

Comparing the Salesperson to the Investigator

Why compare a salesperson to an investigator? The comparison lets you visualize or picture what being a successful salesperson is really like. I'm sure you've noticed actors and actresses on television and in the movies who have played the parts of great investigators. So, what do they do as investigators that salespeople should be doing? Well, for 90 percent of the show, the investigators have very little dialogue. Why?

- They are gathering information without which they cannot solve the case.
- They ask questions and let the suspects do most of the talking.
- They observe their surroundings and the interactions of the other characters.
- They take notes and fit the pieces of the investigative puzzle together, one fact at a time.
- In the end, they give long speeches to show how analyzing the information was important to solving their cases.

Real life detectives do the same. FBI and CIA agents seem to come from the same mold of focused information collectors. I know that being focused is a prerequisite for a detective, and I know that the most successful salespeople are focused information gatherers, too. Like the salesperson, it's the detective's job to focus on asking questions, listening, and observing in order to gain insight. Making others the focus of importance is their objective, and it is quite clear that few veer too far from what it will take to accomplish their goals. They simply continue to ask, listen and observe.

That's what we have to do as salespeople.

> We have to continually focus on asking questions and being effective listeners and observers of our customers.

Fact is, you'll never become a great salesperson without asking questions. It is only through questions that we can gather information, use that information to become problem solvers and help our customers reach their total solutions.

The real key is knowing how to continue to practice the skills of effective questioning,and listening and observing are critical to becoming a top producing salesperson. You can learn as I did, from others who have gone before us in this field. What's that you say? You want me to share with you what I've learned from my mentors and top trainers like Tom Hopkins, Zig Ziglar, Dick Gardner, etcetera? What else? You want to know what corporate leaders say they are looking for in salespeople? I guess you would also like to know what other salespeople who attend my seminars say they took away with them that turned them into selling professionals, right? Now wasn't that easy? All you had to do was ask.

 I'm truly excited to share with you what I have experienced and learned. As you go through the principles in this book, you'll learn what I learned years ago, and you'll have the advantage of doing so in just a fraction of the time. **Ask and you shall achieve!**

What Is Investigative Selling, Anyway?

Investigative selling is really a very simple process that will enable you to dramatically improve your sales performance. Look at the investigators in action. What do they do that salespeople should be doing?

- They **build rapport** through their individual styles of investigative questioning, listening and observing.
- They **gather information** and study it to discover the what, where, why, how and when of the case.

- They use the information gathered and ask more questions to **find total solutions** for the clients.
- They **close the case (sale) and follow up** through a culmination of combined investigative skills.

Do the steps sound familiar? They should! These are the same steps used by a superstar salesperson.

The Investigative Selling Principles I will share with you in this book will teach you how to be the superstar of your own selling career. All you have to do is follow the principles and play the role of a great investigator by doing what they do. Before you know it, you'll be one of the top producers of your company and industry. You'll be achieving your dreams.

How Do I Know the Principles of Investigative Selling Will Work for You?

Let me set your mind at rest. The principles I have written about in this book have worked for me and hundreds of thousands of other salespeople. One of the best ways to demonstrate the power of Investigative Selling was to share with you my own personal story, so if you skipped the Introduction, you may want to go back and read it first. How did I become a self-made millionaire at the age of 31, just nine years after my modest beginning in sales? Simple! I became an investigator—a focused salesperson. I asked questions, gathered information, then used the information to help me become a top producing salesperson in my field.

What Must I Do To Become an Investigative Salesperson?

I have no secret formula or magic wand to turn you into an outstanding investigator; it's up to you. It takes work on your part, but be patient—I'll give you the tools. By owning this book, you have already shown a desire to learn and

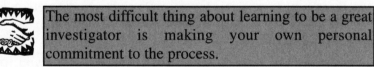

> The most difficult thing about learning to be a great investigator is making your own personal commitment to the process.

a need to discover how to improve your sales performance. Now you must learn the techniques presented in this book, practice them until they feel natural, and be willing to temporarily step outside your comfort zone in selling situations.

> What most average salespeople don't realize is that **it is much tougher to be average than it is to be a superstar salesperson**.

The emotional stress of wanting more, of knowing you are capable but lack the knowledge and skills to get you more, is a trying experience. It makes you want to give up. On the other hand, success gives you a true PASSION for life. All successful salespeople have experienced the rewards of stepping out and taking that chance, of being calculated risk takers. They know that the biggest risk of all is never trying; never reaching their potential because they were afraid to take a chance. What's the risk, anyway? To prove you've learned the lesson, you must take the test! Are you taking a chance by asking questions, listening, observing and practicing all those things that can make you a leading salesperson in your company and your industry? Absolutely not!

So, How Do You Get Started As An Investigator?

Unfortunately, people don't just walk up to you and say, "Hey, you look as though you could use some information. Here, let me tell you everything about me and my company so you can sell me on your offering." Wouldn't that be great? Because this just doesn't happen, we as salespeople have to learn to be better investigators. Therefore, throughout this book you'll learn how to **ask**, not **tell**.

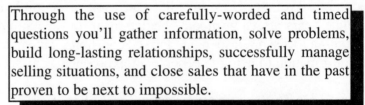

Through the use of carefully-worded and timed questions you'll gather information, solve problems, build long-lasting relationships, successfully manage selling situations, and close sales that have in the past proven to be next to impossible.

And, you'll be enjoying the process. Oh, I forgot one important point. Being an effective investigator is more than just asking; you must **act** on your discoveries.

How do you become a successful investigative salesperson? You learn to become successful by taking that first step, then the next step, and then another and another. It's a step-by-step process to investigative greatness. Make this learning process a memorable experience. Your customers will thank you for it, and your prospects will show their appreciation by owning your offering.

If you are now taking your first step, I would suggest you take notes while learning the Principles of Investigative Selling. In fact, I strongly suggest that you invest in a single notebook that you'll use for note-taking, practice and study of these principles.

How Do Investigative Salespeople Think and Act?

Investigative salespeople think and act like caring professionals. The questioning techniques and strategies I will present in this book are powerful and effective, but if you use them to manipulate or control your selling situations, success will elude you.

- Ask questions because you want to gather the necessary information that will help you offer the most benefits to your prospects.
- Ask questions that will give you insight into the selling situation, then utilize that insight in order to become a problem-solver for your customers.
- Ask questions that enable you to provide added value to your clients, and you'll be establishing relationships that will last throughout your career.

Investigators think and act toward their prospects and customers in ways that make the customers feel most relaxed and comfortable in the selling situation. They think of themselves as educators, teachers, and most of all, as information gatherers. Investigative salespeople think and act respectful, confident of how happy their customers will feel when they own their products and services.

Don't Forget

Most importantly, **investigative salespeople listen more than they talk. They don't act before they have asked all the questions to get the right answers. They continue asking the important questions in order to discover customers' needs, wants and issues.**

What Can You Expect When You Become An Investigative Salesperson?

First of all, you can honestly expect an immediate improvement in your sales performance. What follows that improvement? You'll experience a greater level of production and a substantial increase in income. Like any other positive evolution, one achievement leads to another. When you are no longer preoccupied with money problems, your personal relationships and overall happiness will be that much better, too. You will build your self-image and personal relationships by listening, observing and asking questions that will give you insight into your prospective customer and establish you as a knowledgeable salesperson.

I hope you won't mind a little advice from a self-educated man. If you haven't already developed an investigative library, which holds information about what made the great selling masters successful, I hope this book will be only the first of many in your collection. The top professionals in every field learn and listen to other masters in their field.

- There is a time to learn, and a time to practice and apply what you've learned.
- There is a time to reflect, and get back on course to see what is working and what is not working.
- There is a time to review the selling strategies you may have forgotten. Make the investment in yourself and your business.

> Take the time to become a student first so that you can become the master later.

Then you'll be privileged to help others achieve greatness.

 What Do I Expect From You?

- I expect that you will commit yourself not only just to reading, but also to applying the Principles of Investigative Selling to your selling situations.
- I expect you to share your success with other salespeople who may be going through the struggles and challenges you will have already overcome.
- I expect you to honor the profession of sales by utilizing the principles you will learn in this book with honesty and integrity.
- Lastly, I expect you to surpass your teacher.

Take what I teach you and become a superstar salesperson!

 What Can You Expect From Me?

I want you to know that because you have invested in this book, I'm going to share with you everything I have to teach. I'm going to teach you self-mastery in selling. And when you achieve your dreams, I want to hear your story. I want to celebrate your successes with you.

If you are just beginning in sales, you can look forward to whatever you desire and work hard to achieve. If you have been in selling for a while, and have been unable to reach your goals, I believe your sales will go through the roof. For veteran salespeople who've been around a while and have had some success, I'm going to remind you to do the things that first made you successful, and introduce some new techniques that you'll want to try out for yourself after reading this book.

I must admit, I take your success very personally. Your investment in my book requires of me a personal investment in your future. I will hold back nothing. These principles worked for me and I know they will work for you. Everything I have learned from being a top producer and being with top sales trainers and master salespeople is yours. Success is yours. Just for the asking, you will discover a whole new experience in successful selling. You'll learn how easy successful selling is and why these investigative principles are so effective— whether you're a newcomer to sales or a twenty-year veteran.

When you struggle in your sales career, I share in your struggles and get to work to discover ways to address your challenges in my seminars. When you succeed, I hope to also share in your success by learning from your experiences with the material. In fact, I'll be the first one in line to offer you congratulations. Now that you've decided to be like me, like my father before me, you'll soon recognize yourself as a student who never gives up.

Are you ready to go to the next level and have your sales really take off? Let's go!

SUMMARY POINTS

- Ask and you shall achieve.
- Adopt the character of an investigator by asking questions, gathering information, listening, taking notes, observing and finding total solutions for your customers.
- Don't act like a know it all—ask instead of tell.
- Identify with an investigator and bring those same skills into your sales career.
- By playing the role of investigator, you will always help customers get the total solutions they want by evaluating the facts and clues you have gathered through effective questioning techniques.
- Investigators take notes and fit the pieces of the investigative puzzle together, one fact at a time.
- The actions of an investigative salesperson include . . .
    1. Building rapport through effective questioning, listening and observing.
    2. Gathering information and discovering the what, where, why, when and how.
    3. Using information gathered, asking more questions and finding total solutions.
    4. Closing the sale and practicing effective follow-up.
- One of the most difficult things about learning to be a great investigator is making your own personal commitment to the process.
- It is much tougher to be average than it is to be a superstar salesperson.
- Become a calculated risk-taker. The biggest risk of all is never trying.
- Being an effective investigator is more than just asking; you must ACT on your discoveries.
- Why ask questions?
    1. To gather information that helps you to offer the most benefits to customers.
    2. To give you insight into the selling situation.
    3. To assist you in solving problems and addressing the issues.
    4. To enable you to provide added value to customers.
    5. To help establish a long-lasting relationship.
- Investigative salespeople listen more than they talk.

INVESTIGATIVE PRINCIPLE #2
Get Into Character

CLUE:

Successful People Play Successful Roles

"Acting is a question of absorbing other people's personalities and adding some of your own experience."
Paul Newman

Adopting the character of an investigative salesperson will enable you to build a business foundation of strong customer relationships and outstanding selling skills. Getting into the character of the investigative salesperson is what I do best. It's where my acting and singing background have helped me. Entertaining taught me a lot about selling. In order to get the crowds emotionally involved with my performance, I learned to sell myself AS that character. To create emotional responses to my songs, I had to put everything within me into the song and lose myself in the music.

I have borrowed some of these same strategies I used as a performer and put them to use in this book because they have equipped me to succeed in my selling career. I was more successful than most of my associates at getting my customers emotionally involved in my offering because I played the part—got into the character of the investigator. If I found myself talking too much or not discovering enough information about what it was my clients wanted, I would remind myself to become the investigator and get back into character!

You know what investigative salespeople do better than other types of salespeople, don't you? They take massive action—questioning, listening, observing, prospecting or finding the customers, closing and following up. They investigate. They question. Invest some time in learning to adopt those strategies.

> The questioning techniques set the foundation for the remainder of your selling sequence. It's critical that you master them to stay in character. Through well-developed questioning strategies, you'll be able to deliver a personalized presentation specific to the customer's needs and wants.

To begin the discovery process through proper questioning techniques, it is important to understand all the principles of investigative selling and practice them on a consistent basis. Consistency is the key. The ability to get into and stay in character makes your sales performance consistent. What do I mean by getting into character? Keep reading, my friend. If you examine the truths in this book, take notes, and use the information you gather to improve your selling skills, you are already getting into character.

The great thing about getting into the character of the investigator is that you can pretend to be somebody else for a while. No matter what your day is like, you can leave your challenges at home and turn into the focused problem-solver who is in the investigative selling character. When you have the part down, your customers believe in the new you so much that the time you previously spent persuading them of your worth and competence can now be put to better use. For example, you can ask them about alternative methods they may have tried in order to resolve their current challenges. You may also want to ask them about which of your competitors they have spoken with or plan to speak to about resolving these issues.

Listen and take notes like a good investigator. Decide how you will differentiate yourself and your company from all others, and bring the presentation to a successful close.

> After attempting at least five closes, if you can't close a sale at that particular meeting, listen and take notes in order to use the information you have gathered for future meetings.

When you become an effective listener and note-taker, you'll be prepared to present your case—and deliver a powerful, targeted presentation.

What Does It Take To Be A Successful Salesperson?

It's important to recognize the difference between the words "becoming" and "be." **Becoming** is when you are not there yet. To **be** a successful salesperson, however, requires the continued and consistent behavior that brought you success. Therein lies the challenge. Although it is difficult to learn new selling skills, the true difficulty comes when we are required to sustain those newly learned behaviors or skills for an extended period of time. You must allow yourself to get into character and **"be"** there until you're no longer playing the role of successful salesperson, but the selling skills are a natural part of you. The job of consistent perform then becomes one hundred times easier.

Get Into the Attitude and Style of an Investigative Salesperson

An attitude and style that complements your new character is important. Be confident but not cocky, positive and pleasant without being too sugary, and agreeable without being Mr. or Ms. Wimp. An attitude of dignity is one I usually choose to convey. I know I have an excellent product or service that I believe could be of great benefit to my customers and their companies, so I need to maintain a position as master of the sales process, as the knowledgeable expert in my field. If I begin the presentation begging them to buy, I've lost my winning attitude. It's a pitiful way to sell. I would rather choose another career than have to practice pleading my way into the appointment or sale.

If you are the salesperson you should be, I truly believe you'll have customers calling you as they hear from their peers about how customer-driven you are and how much they like your offerings. Always remember, the customers need and want what you have to sell. If you question the truth of this statement, you are being dishonest with yourself and your customers by trying to sell them something they can't use or don't want. It's an unethical salesperson who sells with slick talk and unrealistic promises, instead of being sensitive to customers' needs. Ethics are a high priority on the superstar salesperson's list. Without them, you have nothing.

Truly successful salespeople earn much more from repeat business and referrals than from the initial sale. Without an ethical sales approach, you will have no repeat business or referrals.

When Do You First Begin Getting Into Character?

If you are going to offer total solutions to your customers' challenges and be the recognized expert in your field, you'll have to research and ask questions first in order to discover their real situations. Depending on the size of your accounts and the type of sales, whether it is a quick one-call sale or a long-term close, you'll want to do a certain amount of research or investigation. Digging up information on your customers is when you first begin getting into the character of an investigator. You may find information on the individual or industry as a whole, or on that one particular company.

> You may find this information in trade journals, your local business journal, library, newspaper or on the Internet. This is the investigative part of your job.

Then you throw yourself right into the role and ASK....

- Ask questions of customers within the organization—those with whom you will be meeting—to determine the hot buttons that will persuade them to do business with you and your company.
- Ask questions of other salespeople within your company who may have met with that company's executives in the past.
- Ask questions of your managers and the leading salespeople within your company, discovering just how they would handle the situation.

Listen to their responses to your questions. Make notes of all the information you gather, and begin to put together your plan or approach.

Profile of an Investigative Salesperson

In order to get into the character of an investigative salesperson, you have to know what the investigative salesperson looks, speaks and acts like. After all, it doesn't matter how much you want to play the role of a sales professional; if you don't know what that role entails, how will you be confident in your own abilities to play the part?

The Successful Investigative Salesperson Looks Like...

A caring, understanding individual who is focused on customer needs and puts people at ease when doing business with them. If you really want to discover what successful salespeople with an investigative eye look like, you might think it would be easiest to simply look in *Forbes Magazine* to see what the typical tycoon wears. Or, look through books, such as *Dress for Success*, for their suggestions on appropriate business attire. While that information can be very helpful, the rules these books and magazines speak of don't always apply to your selling situations.

What is appropriate attire depends on what you sell and to whom you sell it. If your company requires you to call on different sized accounts and speak with different people, you have to be adaptable. If you are in retail sales and have researched the profile of your typical customer, you should dress accordingly. When in doubt, it is always more acceptable to be over-dressed than under-dressed. The success of your sale may depend upon the extent of your investigations.

Instead of letting fashion trends or what you believe to be proper attire dictate your dress, why not discover what will best accommodate your customer? Let me share a story with you. One time I was giving a seminar in Hawaii and came prepared to speak, as always, in my suit. At dinner the evening before, I was advised by the seminar sponsor not to wear a suit. "If you really want to make a hit," Matt said, "get yourself an Aloha shirt and be more casual." I decided to pass the word on to all my staff, from program coordinator to stage setup crew. We all came the next day dressed in Aloha shirts. What an overwhelming welcome we were given; we were totally accepted by the crowd. They knew we had gone out of our way to learn and respect their culture. We had the most successful seminar ever, and helped many companies acquire our products and services to ensure their success.

This process of reflecting the image of what will make your customers most comfortable is known in the business as matching and mirroring. If you are calling on mechanics, a three-piece suit may not be very appropriate. On the other hand, if you were in a meeting with corporate executives, overalls wouldn't be the answer either. The situations aren't always as clear cut as our illustrations, so it's up to you to judge what is acceptable for that particular product and or service. Sometimes all it takes is a word from one of the locals, like my Hawaiian friend.

No matter what the investigative salesperson should look like, the primary focus shouldn't be on the salesperson but on the message. Make your message and its delivery a memorable experience.

From your personal grooming to the car you drive, the briefcase you carry to the paperwork you use, right down to the pen you hand your customer to authorize your agreement, everything should be first-class and clean.

Not long ago my wife, Helen, and I were looking at a new home. We saw a model we liked, and the broker offered to drive us out to the site to get an idea of the view. Well I'll tell you, we couldn't see the view for the distraction of having to sit inside his filthy car. Helen had to climb over toys and scattered paper, and it only got worse in the back seat where I squeezed between bags of empty fast food containers and discarded cans. It was a memorable experience, but perhaps not the memory he wished to leave with us as he said goodbye to the sale and, in our minds, goodbye to his professional image.

The Investigative Salesperson Speaks with...

Confidence and assurance. Investigative salespeople have discovered that slang and profanity have no place in the selling process. Even if customers choose to express themselves in that manner, you should avoid joining them. There are no exceptions. If you maintain a well-mannered presence in the face of loud and over-zealous behavior, you'll always be respected. Your clients will appreciate your stance and even enjoy teasing you once in a while. Remember this little phrase: reserve and preserve—reserve your judgment and preserve your professionalism.

> **Those judged to be the best conversationalist often says very little. What does the investigative salesperson sound like? Much of the time he or she sounds SILENT—listening for clues to close the sale.**

When they do speak, investigative salespeople speak with enthusiasm and energy, getting their customers emotionally involved with their offerings by using emotional words. Draw pictures with your words, and help your prospects to imagine themselves as the proud owners of your product. I'm sure you've all heard the adage "Sell the sizzle instead of the steak." I say, sell the mouth-watering smell of tender, juicy steaks as they slowly drip over a smoky mesquite grill. Sell the warm atmosphere of family and friends gathered around your barbecue, enjoying stories of yesterday and hopes of tomorrow. Sell the feelings of security and love as you clear off the tables, cover the grill and witness the beauty of the orange-red, western sunset from the back yard of your new home. Now that's a picture, don't you think?

Whatever you describe, place your customers in the picture. Let them smell it, taste it, feel it, hear it, and see it through your words. Whatever the product and service, the investigative salesperson manages to get clients to use their imaginations.

- How will they look owning it?
- How will they feel using it?
- What will they hear others say about them because they own it?
- What differences will they experience because they are the
  smart owners of your offering?

Once you learn to speak in descriptive pictures that capture the imagination and excitement of your prospects, they'll learn to picture themselves owning. It really depends on your ability to be a good storyteller. The better the story, the greater your chances are of selling the star of your story—your product or service. Manage your customers and master the selling situation to the mutual benefit of all parties. Your investigations will reveal so much about your clients, they will feel like close friends of the family. They'll trust you to give them the best advice, which will generate long-term relationships and give you referrals.

Between Speaking and Acting Lies Nonverbal Language
Comfort levels, product and service preferences, and some feelings and beliefs are often expressed using nonverbal language. The prospect may be saying one thing, but their body language could be delivering a completely different message. Volumes have been written about the advantages of reading the messages sent through body language. It really takes an aware person to distinguish negative from positive signals. Some people call this reading between the lines. At first, you may be too preoccupied just trying to get through the presentation and answer the objections. However, soon you'll want to study these nonverbal clues and respond accordingly. When you learn about body language, you'll discover that your gestures are being read as well. Are you paying attention to what you're saying, nonverbally?

You should never underestimate those to whom you are offering your product and service. They could be excellent readers of nonverbal language and be taking in your every move. If your voice is patient and your attitude seems positive, but your arms are closely folded across your chest and your lips are pursed, the observant customer will know you're not as understanding as you sound.

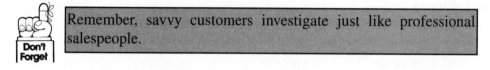

Remember, savvy customers investigate just like professional salespeople.

A Successful Investigative Salesperson Acts with...

A passionate HUNGER for success. That hunger is critical to becoming successful! This is easy to have when you believe wholeheartedly in your product and service. If you don't believe in your product, you should choose one that does stir your blood and get you excited. To persuade, you must have product hunger. You should also be hungry to become the best investigative salesperson in your company or industry. If you have an insatiable hunger to succeed, the rejection won't put out your flame; it will only fuel your fire.

Top producers also have a dislike for that dirty word—average! Because they perceive themselves as exceptional, they become their perception. Let me say that again because those last few words are some of the most important you may ever hear.

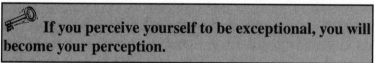

If you perceive yourself to be exceptional, you will become your perception.

The opposite holds true as well. If you perceive yourself to be incapable of successful selling, chances are you'll fulfill that prophecy. The lesson to be learned is to act confident and believe in yourself and be driven to perform better than your competition. Act as if it was impossible to fail and positive things will be attracted to you.

Once You Get Into Character, Develop Investigative Behaviors That Will Keep You There

Just like I had to do, you'll probably have to break some bad habits you've developed over the years. Here's one instance when the novice salesperson definitely has the advantage over the seasoned veteran; they haven't had much time to develop and reinforce bad habits.

One of the most difficult habits to break, and the biggest contributor to sales suicide, is what we discussed in Chapter One—**telling** instead of **asking**.

Customers don't really want to know what <u>you</u> think they want; they want you to listen to what <u>they</u> believe are their needs, wants and issues. If you want to know how Tom and Mary buy, you better put yourself in Tom and Mary's hide! If you want to know how John Doe buys, you have to see through John Doe's eyes.

Asking about and listening to the customer's response is especially difficult for those of you who love to talk.

The closings you'll find the most strained will be when you must close your lips. When you've mastered that closing with the techniques I'll teach you, you'll be well on your way to achieving greatness in sales.

Although some habits are good, many of the mechanical and automatic things we do each day have the ability to open doors to unconscious habits that may have drastic results on your selling career. We are creatures of habit, so let's turn bad habits into good. Actually, I'm so picky about the unconscious development of bad sales habits that I avoid the seemingly meaningless, everyday habits that have nothing to do with selling. One habit leads to another.

- I don't put on my pants, shoes and socks in the same order every day.
- I don't shave the same side of my face first every morning.
- I don't drink from the same coffee cup.
- I even change my workout routine every three months.

Sounds silly, I know, but I want to be able to stay fresh and change as needed to achieve my goals.

There have been times when I've kept my mind and eyes open to new ideas and concepts, and been able to make minor adjustments to my usual way of doing things that brought about even greater success. What you want to do in sales is forget the word habit. The definition of habit includes the word routine. What I'm talking about is establishing a conscious behavior, a purposefully chosen behavior versus an unconscious one. Design a planned, systematic behavior that has a proven track record for success. Behaviors won't create static boredom such as habit or routine suggests; instead, they'll give you security. When you're asked a common question in selling, about your product and service, that you've been asked a hundred times before, you'll feel secure responding with that favorite answer that has brought you so much success. Don't get so stuck on it that you aren't open to seeking ways to improvement.

> It's not about habit! It's about behaviors and practices that have proven to be successful in the past and are eagerly applied to similar situations in anticipation of similar results.

When you are making that first call on a prospective client, habit can make your voice sound hum-drum and drab; whereas, awareness combined with an established routine assures you of a greater chance to schedule a meeting because you're familiar with how the situation is most likely to develop.

Okay, back to the behaviors. Well-established, positive behaviors assure you a greater chance to schedule a meeting because you're familiar with the behavior that brought you previous success. Don't let that presentation that you've given time after time let you fall into the habit of monotone speaking and unenthusiastic gestures. Let your success routines bring renewed excitement and energy to your voice and movements because chances are you are leaving that meeting with new business!

One of the unconscious habits I used to have was very detrimental for my speaking career, but slipped by me unnoticed until Tom Murphy pointed it out to me. Almost every other sentence began or ended with a "you know." I hadn't realized how much those two annoying words had become a part of my speech; they had crept right in when I least expected them, you know? You know, they were the most difficult two words to get rid of. It took a real friend, you know, to help me correct the problem. Isn't that the most irritating habit? I made an agreement to pay Murph a dollar each time I said "you know." It cost me $50 before I got the "you know" habit out of my vocabulary.

Don't Forget

Keep in mind, it takes time to develop and perfect good new habits or routines. It also takes patience with yourself and the willingness to get back on track when you have let yourself slide into those old ways. Good selling instincts aren't developed overnight. Through diligence and desire, however, you can replace bad habits with great routines.

In my early days of selling, I was introduced to the studies of a renowned surgeon, Dr. Maxwell Maltz.   Dr. Maltz developed Psycho-Cybernetics and discovered through his studies that it takes twenty-one days of changed behavior to make or break a habit.   When his amputee patients complained of having itches on limbs they no longer possessed, or reaching for objects with hands that had been amputated, he realized that the mind of these patients had not yet internalized the loss.   Why?   It takes approximately twenty-one days in order for the brain to catch up with the behavior.   So it is with good habits as well.

> It takes approximately twenty-one days of consistent investigative practice to feel comfortable with the principles.

Be patient with yourself when getting into the character of the investigative salesperson, and be careful to make positive choices that keep you in character. Resist the urge to **tell**.   Practice **observing, asking questions, and actively listening.**   Easier said than done, right?   We tell when we should ask!   We talk when we should listen!   Keep in mind: as much as you want to feel important and show your prospects what you know, they are anxiously awaiting their turn to do the same.

> Resist the temptation to be entertaining to your customers; instead, give them the opportunity to entertain you with their stories, their dreams and their goals.   Just keep on investigating by asking, listening, observing and taking notes.

I hope you have noticed by now that controlling the conversation doesn't always mean you are the one to do all the talking.   The best way to control the conversation is by asking questions and actively listening to the answers like a good investigator.   Actually, I prefer using the word "manage" instead of control, because control creates such a negative picture.   You have to be forever conscious of the pictures and perceptions you create with your words.   When I think of managing the conversation, I think of all aspects of communication, including asking questions, actively listening, observing body language, offering feedback, and building a relationship through mutual respect.   When I think of control, on the other hand, I think of an adversarial relationship, a power struggle, manipulating tactics. Some salespeople believe they must control; I believe you should manage.

Along With Investigative Behaviors, What About the Strategies You'll Need?

Investigative strategies offer opportunities for greater achievement. As you continue studying the strategies of investigative selling, you'll begin to recognize the attributes of successful salespeople. You'll also become an information gatherer who truly listens and is interested in the customer's concerns. You'll develop internal instincts of observation, allowing you insight into other transactions. You'll graduate to a higher level of communication where your words are carefully selected to encourage emotional involvement and excitement. Through it all, you'll be an efficient time manager. Your professionalism will make you a calculated risk-taker and a man or woman of action who can creatively hold together the most challenging selling situation.

The results will be a perfect ending more times than not. Say goodbye to the typical sales slumps you may have experienced in the past.

When you see your performance start to slide, you'll know you must get back in character. Ask questions—listen—observe—take notes—close. In doing so, you'll experience greater sales volume and have a lot more fun achieving your professional goals.

Rewards of Being A Professional Salesperson

As a professional investigative salesperson, you'll find yourself learning from everyone you come in contact with. Here are just a few of the wonderful things you'll learn:

From Sales Leaders & Trainers	**From Customers & Prospects**
✔ Learned about their success	✔ Learned about clients' success
✔ Observed success surroundings	✔ Observed clients' surroundings
✔ Listened with intent	✔ Listened with intent
✔ Gathered information for success	✔ Gathered information for sale
✔ Asked questions	✔ Asked questions
✔ Followed their example	✔ Followed up with clients' needs
✔ Kept in touch with mentors	✔ Developed ongoing communication
✔ Continued my education in sales	✔ Continued learning about clients

Now That You Know What Getting Into Character Is, How Do You Stay There?

You stay in character by continuing the behavior that got you there in the first place. It's an ongoing process. This should go without saying, but just in case it needs to be mentioned, I thought it better to cover the subject. There are some simple selling rules that apply to almost every situation.

- Don't chew gum.
- Don't play with your mustache.
- Don't adjust your clothing.
- Don't smoke during face-to-face contact with a customer.

If you do, you'll undo all the good that you gathered from your investigations. Try to minimize any nervous behaviors that could be considered offensive to customers.

Much of your behavior is unconscious, so how do you change behavior you don't know you have? One way is to video or audio tape one of your sales presentations. You don't have to do this with a real customer. Have your spouse or friend sit through a practice run. That's what will help you to stay in character once you get there. As a matter of fact, looking or listening to yourself on tape might be the best entertainment you and your friends have had for quite a while.

Even if you consider yourself quite polished, you'll be amazed at all the extra words you may have added to your presentation, making it long and somewhat boring. You also won't believe the times you failed to make eye contact with your client, the reactions your clients had that you failed to capitalize on, and the times you may have repeated negatives or addressed objections that weren't really true objections after all. If you discover all those areas that need improvement when you know you are being taped and are on your best behavior, can you imagine what your regular presentation might be like?

Consistency In Investigative Sales Puts You In the "Selling Zone"®

If you play the investigative role successfully, you will find yourself in the Selling Zone. What is the Selling Zone? It's that incredible place where you are selling at your highest peak. It's call after call that ends perfectly because of your talented execution. That's when selling isn't a job. It's a whole lot of fun. Don't be fooled, it's not a place totally free of disappointments, professional setbacks and personal struggles. However, the Selling Zone is crowded with other elite investigative salespeople who have managed to survive this exciting business we call sales and actually enjoy the experience. They have learned to turn their failures into learning experiences, look at every "no" as one step closer to that big transaction, and face rejection with a sense of humor and a winning attitude.

> The professionals who populate the Selling Zone have maintained their dignity during the sale. They have positioned themselves as knowledgeable experts in their field, and they are more than happy to help newcomers learn to do the same.

The best kept secret in sales is that there is really no secret to success at all, except hard work and more hard work. These professionals realize that when salespeople slump, it is normally because they have drifted away from the fundamentals in sales, away from playing the role of investigative salesperson. They have stepped out of character.

Don't be counted as one of those salespeople. Learning these investigative principles is going to increase your production levels and spur you on to even greater accomplishments.

SUMMARY POINTS

- Being an investigative salesperson allows you to be somebody else for a while. You can leave your self-conscious, shy self at home during the meeting.
- Get into the attitude and style of an investigative salesperson.
- Avoid unconscious habits; it takes twenty-one days to make or break a habit. Think of exchanging habits for planned, systematic routines of proven successful sales results.
- Don't make **you** be the issue. What your customers should remember is your ability to serve.
- Make sure your sales language is positive and know when to be quiet and listen.
- Observe nonverbal body language. Sometimes the verbal and nonverbal language will deliver two different messages.
- Being an investigative salesperson is an ongoing strategy, not an end result.
- Consistency in investigative sales puts you in the "Selling Zone."

INVESTIGATIVE PRINCIPLE #3
Develop the Investigative Instinct---Listen & Observe

CLUE:

The More You Talk The Less You Earn

"Customers will tell you how they want to be sold. All you must do is listen."

Omar Periu

We spoke in Chapter Two about the need to break some bad habits. The areas most salespeople needed to focus on and improve in are their listening and observation skills. Much of your success in sales can be attributed to having outstanding listening and observation skills because the ultimate goal of listening is understanding. The investigator who talks all the time won't discover the information needed to solve the case. How long do you think an investigator will be on the job with open files that have no solutions? Not long? The clients needing answers will find another investigator to serve them. The same holds true for salespeople.

> Those who are too busy telling instead of asking probably won't be in sales very long.

Unfortunately, they'll blame their "go-nowhere" selling status on the economy or some other acceptable excuse instead of seeking out methods of self-improvement. It has been my experience that many people who say they can't sell should really rethink the situation. Chances are, the true difficulties lie with listening and observing the selling situations. If this is the case with you, don't give up on selling just yet. Being a good listener and observer can be learned.

In order to learn these skills, you must first be able to identify what constitutes a good, or active listener. Being a good listener sounds easy in theory, but in practice it's a whole different ball game. Believe it or not, there is a lot more energy involved in listening than in talking. You have to set aside what it is you want to say and focus on what others have to contribute. And, there is also a big difference between kicking back and daydreaming and practicing **active** listening skills.

Since I've been discussing the importance of avoiding the habit of **telling** your customers, I've decided to follow my own advice and show you instead of tell you what active listening is and is not.

Active listening <u>is</u>

- leaning forward slightly with a focused look in your eye.
- making eye to eye contact.
- jotting down notes about what you think and speaking those points later if they are not covered by others.
- nodding agreement and interjecting a "You're right!" "I see!" "I agree!" or "I understand." comment now and then to show you're paying attention.
- asking for clarification on something you don't understand.
- repeating back important points to confirm what was said.
- understanding that what you have to hear is most of the time more important than what you have to say.
- staying in character.

Active listening is <u>not</u>

- glazed eyes gazing off into the distance.
- pen poised above a sheet of paper you have been staring at for the last hour.
- irritated tapping of feet or pen while somebody else talks.
- reviewing in your mind what you have to do back at the office.
- planning in your mind how you will respond to that last comment.
- taking a mental vacation.

One of the first things you should do is identify what is inhibiting your ability to listen well. It's funny, but once you become a better listener, being more aware of your surroundings seems to come almost naturally.

Let's work on pinpointing some of the poor listening habits you may have fallen into over the years and determine what needs to be done to break those habits.

Effective Listening Test

1. Are you often preoccupied with other ideas and suggestions floating around in your mind while someone else is trying to deliver a message or communicate a problem? Does this make it almost impossible for you to focus on what that other person is trying to say?

2. Do you practice the old "you start the sentence and I'll finish it" routine when someone is talking to you at a much slower pace than you usually speak?

3. Do you often react to a challenge or conflict by speaking your mind before you've heard from all involved parties?

4. Are you nervous and hesitant when meeting with others you consider to be in an authoritative position, so you are constantly planning your next words while the other is speaking?

5. After you have gained the specific information you need from an individual, do you find his or her additional input unnecessary and proceed to tune them out?

6. After you have contributed your expertise during a meeting, do you find it more entertaining to kick back and daydream while your peers participate in the meeting?

7. If you have asked a pointed question and the person answering feels the need to go off topic a bit, do you impatiently remind them of the question or do you enjoy the wandering and hope to pick up some insightful information you hadn't thought to ask?

8. Do you feel uncomfortable asking clarifying questions during a conversation you have found difficult to understand?

9. If you see confused looks on the faces of others in the room after you have delivered important information, do you avoid asking anyone if they have questions because you fear you won't have the answers?

10. When someone is speaking on a subject you know a great deal about, do you feel the need to enthusiastically jump in with your views and opinions?

How did you do? If you answered "yes" to one or more of these questions, it may be costing you a great deal of money in sales. So let's see how, together, we can help you to attain the investigator's instinct and become an active listener instead of a selective one.

I hope your responses to the test were honest and opened your eyes to what has caused you to close your ears. Once you recognize what needs improving, it is just a matter of putting yourself in those situations and practicing good listening skills. The more you learn to listen to what others have to say, the more you'll begin to value their contributions.

> When people feel valued, they'll reveal all kinds of information that will help you with your investigative selling strategies.

In Chapter Two, I talked a lot about how to get into character and stay in character for consistent sales results. One very important way you can stay in character is by asking questions; it's really not difficult. Soon you'll discover some truths about your customers, and they'll think you are a wonderful conversation when all you've done is listen to their needs. They'll know you care because you are informed about their company and have done your homework well, when, in actuality, they have told you all you needed to know and you've simply practiced feedback and repeated the learned information. In other words, they'll believe and trust you because you unselfishly took the time to listen, observe and learn.

How to Become an Active Listener
Get **FOCUSED**!

F eed back concepts to acknowledge the speaker and clarify possible misunderstandings.

O bserve the speaker's body language. He or she may be delivering conflicting messages.

C ontrol your emotions. Manage the volume, tone and pitch of your voice.

U se gestures to demonstrate active listening skills. Then customers know you're tuned in.

S tructure and organize your thoughts before responding. Meaningful pauses are okay.

E liminate internal and external distractions and maintain eye contact.

D on't interrupt the speaker. Be patient and hear him or her out.

Listening Is an Emotional Experience

At first, when you are struggling with poor listening habits, you will still be quite preoccupied with self-talk. You know what I mean—the words you say to yourself when you are trying to hold back a response or hone in on a conversation that may be less than inspiring. You may be having such an inner battle with yourself that much of the external conversation is lost in the process, but keep up the good fight. Your clients will never know of the silent process going on inside your mind. They'll think that wrinkled brow and concerned look on your face is studied interest in what they're saying. Just keep practicing until active listening becomes a natural process for you.

How I Learned To Be an Active Listener!

Because of my background as a young boy from Cuba with no English language skills, being an active listener was a dire necessity for me. From the moment I entered school, I had to listen with my whole being because English was my second language. Spanish was my primary language. For years I would think my sentences through in Spanish first and then translate them into English. All through school I felt stupid, almost incapable of learning simply because I couldn't speak the language. I was actually put back after my first year in school.

During the primary grades the words I heard meant little to me. The further behind I got, the quieter I became. When I started having some knowledge of the English language, I was so far behind in school that the feeling of stupidity persisted. People didn't understand me, so why bother to understand them, I thought. Most of the time my friends thought I was shy, when in reality it was feelings of inferiority that held me back.

I loved to talk at home, speaking the language I knew: Spanish. That was my comfort zone. I had to really work hard at learning this difficult language, English, which was being spoken in school. The only way to understand it was to listen to each word intently and watch their lips form the words. I became accustomed to reading the speaker's expressions and body language so I could understand what teachers and friends were trying to say to me.

This went on throughout my years in elementary school. One day in eighth grade it all paid off. What happens to most boys about that time, definitely happened to me—I discovered GIRLS. For the first time, they were speaking my language without even opening their mouths. I had become so accustomed to actively listening and reading body language, it was no trouble for me to understand that they were as interested as I was.

One girl in particular had won my heart; I suffered a severe case of puppy love. I was compelled to communicate my feelings to her. It was the first time I realized the importance of being thought of as the independent, silent type. Although I didn't identify our nonverbal language as speaking and reading body language, that was exactly what we did. We spoke and listened with our entire souls—our eyes, our lips and our hearts were all involved. What I had been doing all those years to learn and understand English, listening intently with all my being, was finally bringing me positive results.

Take this out of the romantic setting and that is exactly what we have to do when we are in front of a customer. We need to listen intently with all our beings.

You won't have to wait near as long as I did to see positive results. As it should be in a relationship, stay focused on being the giver. Give the speaker your full, undivided attention.

> Actively listen by making eye contact, observing body language and expressing nonverbal and verbal agreement to what is being said. Give others the opportunity to express their ideas and suggestions.

The only thing you should be taking is the time to listen, observe and reflect on the information you are gathering by being an active listener and an information gatherer.

I was once told by a great trainer, Dick Gardner, "You don't have to tell me how you feel, Omar. Your actions are so LOUD they are deafening!" He was referring to my use of my whole being while conversing with others. I consider that a great compliment!

Being receptive to what others have to say makes them feel important, and the lines of communication will remain open. Customers will tell you how to sell them; all you have to do is listen. Constant interruptions in a conversation will soon discourage other contributions, and you'll find yourself in a one-way conversation leading nowhere. Suddenly, communication is canceled due to lack of interest! When you become a better listener, you'll find yourself wondering what the more quiet people are thinking about and encourage them to become involved in the conversation by asking about their thoughts. That's when everybody benefits.

Listen, Learn and Translate What You Hear

Now that you are listening more and gathering much more information, what does every effective investigative salesperson do with it all? First, you must distinguish between what is important and what is not. This can be done most effectively if you are a good note-taker. Note-taking is a real plus to your selling career.

> People like doing business with detail-oriented people, and you will demonstrate that trait by being a good note taker.

There are several ways to use the notes you have taken during a meeting.

(1) You may want to save the notes to look at when the information isn't as fresh. What doesn't seem important directly after a meeting could be of paramount importance weeks down the road when you're preparing your presentation.

(2) Sometimes you will have to look back at your notes to verify what was promised to your customers. Just the act of writing things down will help you to remember them. Keeping good notes will give you a storehouse of information at your fingertips. When you review your notes at a later date, you may pick up on something that failed to capture much of your attention the first time around.

(3) Sometimes in the thick of conversation, you may fail to identify important trigger words that give you a reason to get back with the customer or to pursue a different avenue or a more effective approach at your next meeting.

For example, let's say you're selling cars. A young couple visits your location to "just look" at a great looking sport utility vehicle they saw on the street. You, of course, are pleasant and help them as much as you can. You ask a lot of questions and take a lot of notes. They return a week later and ask for you because you were so nice and gave them your card. In reviewing your notes, you see that they had mentioned getting a little camper trailer as well. You mention this early in your second conversation and they're impressed. You also present them with a vehicle with a towing package and possibly a bigger engine than what they had looked at last week. Your notes are helping you help them to get just what they need!

An investigative salesperson's greatest tool is learning what will motivate a prospective client to own his or her offering. Those needs are often hidden between the lines. Reviewing your notes helps you to narrow in on what features or benefits of your products or services will persuade prospective clients to own.

Taping the conversation can also be very helpful, and it eliminates the distraction of taking notes during the conversation. A word of caution, though! Always ask permission to tape, and explain to them that you want to make sure that what you promised to deliver will be remembered once you get back to the office. Make them see it as a benefit, not something to be concerned about. A great thing about tape recorders is that, unlike most humans, they don't practice selective listening. This doesn't mean you shouldn't write down things on your notepad, though, but you can relax a bit if you are taping. Take notes of the most important details needed to make the right decision for your customers.

Does Stumbling Over Your Ego Keep You From Being A Good Listener?

Nobody ever believes this to be true about him/herself, but, sadly for many, it is a fact. When your ego gets in the way it is difficult to listen to what others are saying because you are too busy listening to yourself. We all have a desire to be heard. Don't let your ego override your desire to listen. If you do, your sales income will be severely limited.

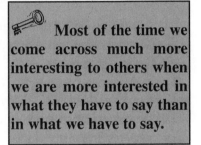

Most of the time we come across much more interesting to others when we are more interested in what they have to say than in what we have to say.

It's been said that listening is the active demonstration of interest in another person. However, it can require a great deal of patience on your part if the conversation is incredibly interesting and you want to jump in or, on the flip side, if it is so boring you could take a nap and not miss anything worth mentioning. Still you must set aside your ego. Believe me when I tell you, there are times when people experience the same feelings about your conversations!

In many cases, it's your ego that makes you talk too much and butt in too often. You need to keep your ego in check if you don't want to be the recipient of rolled eyes and long sighs whenever you begin a conversation. Break the habit of breaking in on conversations. Few people will mind if you listen and enjoy, but it can cause resentment when you feel the need to constantly dominate conversations in which you were not initially invited to participate. The next time you want to join in a conversation, make it a point to be silent and listen. Be the investigator. Listen and observe other people. You'll learn things about them you never realized, simply by closing your mouth and opening your ears. When you're not so busy expounding, you'll be able to identify others' likes and dislikes, their wants and needs. What a great advantage you will have when you listen and observe, and you'll begin to see continuous growth and consistent improvement in your sales performance.

Investigative salespeople know that listening and observing will help them in both their personal and professional lives. It's the novice who worries about how they'll ever get to tell the customer about their offering if all they ever do is listen! The point is—you won't **tell** them at all. The beauty of being a good listener is that you lead the customer to where you want them to be by skillfully questioning and actively listening. Instead of you telling them what they need, they'll be asking for your advice. Then, they'll think the whole idea of owning your offering was theirs in the first place.

More Experienced Salespeople Have More Listening Challenges

That's why you need to become an effective investigator. The listening process is a difficult one, and it doesn't get much easier with time unless you equip yourself with the necessary tools of active listening. I am speaking from experience. The more sales experience I had, the more difficult it was to listen to the customer, to hear them out. Why? Because experience taught me the common customer objections and challenges, and I was more than prepared with all the answers. I had confidently identified most of the challenges and felt able to overcome almost any objection. So, instead of making myself hear the customer out, I would interrupt with answers to those concerns that had worked well for me in the past. Bad strategy!

The one thing we experienced salespeople forget is that we don't know everything. The only way to understand your prospects is to treat them as individuals rather than members of a typical group. Respect the fact that they need to voice their individual concerns, and that those concerns may be quite different from the previous twenty-five calls you made where customers have said the exact same thing.

> **Listen to your customer. Hear him or her out. When you do, your chances for consummating the sale are dramatically increased and your opportunity to step up the customer order with added value or benefits is many times greater.**

Investigators Practice Patience, and Patience Pays Off

One way to teach yourself to become an active listener is to think of it in terms of dollars earned. Every time you practice great listening and observation skills, make it money in the bank. One of my students, Michael, approached me after one of my seminars and shared this story with me about how he perfected his listening skills.

Michael had attended a previous seminar and had heard my message about how sales figures would climb in direct proportion to listening and observation skills. He went into the office the next day and decided to launch an all out campaign to become a better listener.

To help him stay **FOCUSED** he decided he would do what I had recommended. That very day he began to take notes when his customers spoke and made it a point to review his notes with them in order to clarify their needs and/or concerns. Not only did this help him during later presentations, but he shared with me how his follow-up calls became very **FOCUSED** as well. Most of his clients were so impressed with what he remembered about their previous conversations that they didn't hesitate to schedule follow-up meetings. Michael made his customers feel valued by being an effective investigator.

He also shared with me how much time he saved by simply recapping important points and avoiding addressing old objections that had already been answered. At the end of that year, Michael's productivity had increased by 60 percent and he went on to purchase his own business. I'm sure you'll agree, it wasn't difficult for Michael to recognize the dollar value of investigative selling.

Michael learned what many top sales professionals already know. He learned to listen and to take notes as well. Listening just isn't enough if you are making multiple sales calls in one day and gathering a tremendous amount of information. Notes are definitely necessary for follow-up. In fact, it's a good idea to go over the important points with a highlighter at the end of each meeting, so you won't waste a lot of time on things that prove unnecessary to a successful close. These highlighted points will end up being the key elements of a successful close when you return with your solutions or closing presentation.

What About Observation Skills?

Combine listening with observation skills and everybody wins! Ultimately, your goal is not just to become a better listener, but to translate the importance of what you hear and to understand what impact that information can have on ensuring a successful close. However, if you are to maximize your encounters with customers, observation skills must be developed too. Think of it as hearing with your whole being. When you walk into your customers' offices, they are telling you something about themselves through their furnishings, color selections, pictures, awards on display, desk and seating arrangements, books and whatever else they may find important enough to have around them during the day.

By being observant and looking at pictures on their desks, perhaps you'll discover whether they are married and have children. Looking around at what may be hung on their walls might tell you what their hobbies are, or perhaps the extent of their community involvement. You'll also notice if they are orderly and well organized or if you'll have to double check their receipt of your product. If they have a conference table in their office but choose to separate themselves behind the desk, that may be an indication of how they are feeling about this meeting.

When you are open to observing the physical surroundings and personal signals of your customers, you'll be making mental, as well as written, notes before that customer ever begins the conversation.

Practice Makes Perfect

There is an easy way to practice observation skills without ever letting people know what you are doing. When you leave a restaurant or a social gathering at a friend's home, see if you can picture the surroundings. Try to remember colors, pictures, furnishings, anything that might give you some insight into their personality. Now, when you have remembered as much as you can, ask yourself how that information can be translated into discovering details about those who may work or live there. Why might they feel comfortable in these surroundings? What does this say about them? Keep asking those investigative questions, even if they are silent ones within your mind. Now that you have made mental notes, when possible, jot down on a note pad the items that will help you build rapport and make the sale.

On a call with a client, continue to ask those silent questions to yourself during the observation process. Ask yourself what possible significance that poster hanging over the credenza may have. If it is a picture of a special event, maybe they were there or wish they had been able to attend. If it's a sports figure, maybe they are into that sport or personally know the athlete. If it's a framed poem or quote, it could give you insight into their philosophy. Maybe it has no specific importance other than the colors worked well with the furnishings. Whatever the reason, it's a great exercise in observation and can help you build rapport with your customers.

Listening and Observing When the Heat is On

It can be difficult to listen and observe during ideal situations, but what about when the pressure's on? What happens when you are facing the challenges of a crowded room or the expectations of upper-level executives? All those old habits you thought were conquered could possibly come back with a vengeance, couldn't they? Whatever you do, don't panic. It's a good thing to practice improving your observation skills under less than ideal situations in order to challenge yourself with tougher assignments. I thought I was doing just that, challenging myself to listen even when I didn't feel anything important was being said. I learned quite differently in the following situation.

During my years as a professional singer, some of the band members and I would go to the local retirement homes and perform for free. The residents enjoyed the music quite a bit, but what they liked even more than the singing was the opportunity to talk to someone.

After the performances, I welcomed the conversation of some of those older folks. You know what I discovered? I found out that I didn't know everything after all. I enjoyed the opportunity to speak with them about their experiences even more than they enjoyed talking with me. They had the best stories, some of which I still use in my seminars. By listening and observing, I discovered little "gems" of information that made me stop and look at the situation in a different way. Their conversations are so valuable to me because now I know why they have lived so long and experienced so much—in order to pass all their insight on to us young pups who think we know it all.

Although that wasn't really a selling situation, it taught me a lot about listening when the heat is on and the interest is off in different selling situations. Those are the times when you both need to and hate to listen the most.

If you think you have heard your sales manager deliver the same old tired speech, try listening once again. You may be surprised at those little "gems" you pick up along the way.

Sometimes when the heat is on and you're too close to the flame, you need to listen with an open mind and understanding heart. Put yourself in the place of the person who may be a bit angry or upset. Ask yourself what your contribution was to create this situation, and what you can personally do to make things right. When you listen with understanding and sensitivity to the other person's concerns, that caring attitude comes across in your expression and words.   W h e n all is said and done, voicing your responsibility for the problem goes a long way in cooling down the "hot" situation.

During these times your notes may not be so much about what the other person said, but about what comes into your mind as the probable cause and solution. By the time the customer or executive is through venting, you may have come up with a plausible solution because you listened with an open mind. Instead of planing to get even or get out of there, you were planning to get a handle on what could be done to rectify the situation.

Believe this, keeping a cool head and an open-minded attitude will be looked upon as a mature way to resolve conflict.

> When you listen and then ask for a customer's suggestions and input on what would help them in the situation, you are the one in control of the conversation. You are managing like an investigator. When you leave, it will be on a positive note, equipped with the information you need to improve your sales performance and productivity.

Once You've Listened and Observed, It's Time To Respond!

When the selling situation does get rather heated, good salespeople know the words to say that will let the steam out, nice and easy. There are specific words that help to relieve pressure situations. Although we'll cover this in more detail when we discuss objections, I thought it might be helpful to throw a few in now to put your mind at rest. The following are a few examples of words and phrases that help to relieve the pressure and avoid conflict during a selling situation.

Prospect: "Your company failed to deliver what the last salesperson promised. I'm not about to make the same mistake and put my faith in you again!"

Salesperson: "I totally <u>understand</u> your <u>feelings</u>. If I were you I'd feel the same way and because of that I would like to have your permission to <u>ask</u> a few questions so I can discover just where the breakdown took place. You see, Mr. Prospect, that particular salesperson is no longer with our company, and I suspect he was let go for just that reason. <u>May I</u> assume you would be <u>understanding</u> enough to not judge our entire company by one poor representative?"

Right away the salesperson reduced the pressure by letting the prospect know his/her feelings were understood. Then the salesperson respectfully asked permission to ask questions. Lastly, the salesperson focused on the fact that he or she knew the customer would be fair and understanding and would not judge every representative by that one bad experience.

Prospect: "No way are we going to pay that much money. I believe your company is simply asking way too high a price."

Salesperson: "I understand how you feel, Mr. Prospect! Or, "I couldn't agree with you more, Mr. Prospect!" Or, "I can appreciate your feelings, Mr. Prospect!" In fact XYZ Corporation felt the same way you do until its production levels increased by more than 20 percent and their quality control remained just as effective. Just how much too much do you feel our product is?"

Just by saying those two few words of understanding in response to the customer's rising concern, the salesperson was able to validate the customer's feelings, letting him or her know the point was well understood, yet provided proof that there was reason to still consider owning the offering. The next step would be to move on to clarify the objection. Can you see how learning some pressure-releasing words and phrases can encourage the customer to continue the meeting? You'll learn more about these phrases that I call "Reflex Responses" in a following chapter.

Listening Persistence Is Another Key to Opening Doors In the Investigative Selling Process

Persistence is the name of the game. You may not make immediate discoveries, and you may not make immediate improvements. Listening, observing, gathering, translating, and utilizing learned information is a long and continual process. It may require researching your customers, planning a presentation strategy, listening to what your peers have to contribute, being observant and learning from it all.

Sometimes you think you know your customer backward and forward and go into the meeting only to discover another person has replaced him or her, or the meeting has been canceled all together. That's when you take what you've learned and apply it to similar selling situations in the future. Sometimes no matter what you've done and how well you've listened, the response just isn't what you expected.

The way I see it, when this happens you have two choices:
1. You can give up
2. Dig in and plan another route to your final destination.

Those who give up probably won't be in sales for long. Those of us who dig in with an alternative route have the fortitude to succeed even under the most adverse conditions. We're the investigative salespeople who will continue for years being involved in sales careers that we enjoy and find extremely prosperous.

There's one thing about being a successful salesperson—when you understand the principles of investigative selling, you have a great time listening to the excitement your product and service creates in your customer. You find yourself empowering others, like Michael, who discovered the wonders of owning his own business. All you have to do is believe in your product and service and feel confident of the benefits your customers will receive when they own your offering. For good investigators, the selling will continue throughout their lives and will be the most rewarding profession in the world.

Now that you have a better understanding of how to listen, observe, ask questions, gather information and become a more effective investigator, start applying those skills in all your selling situations. That's what will make the reading of this book so valuable—immediate application of your newly learned skills. Read, learn, then practice what you've learned. This very day make an active decision to become the investigator in all your selling situations.

SUMMARY POINTS

- The more you talk, the less you earn.
- Get **focused** on active listening.

> **F**eed back concepts to acknowledge speaker and clarify message.
>
> **O**bserve nonverbal communications.
>
> **C**ontrol your emotions.
>
> **U**se natural gestures to demonstrate active listening.
>
> **S**tructure thoughts before speaking.
>
> **E**liminate distractions.
>
> **D**on't interrupt.

- Keep customer needs first—-get your ego out of the way..
- Hear your customers out and provide added value for them and you.
- Take notes and highlight key points during the questioning process.
- Apply what you are learning in this book to today's selling situations.

INVESTIGATIVE PRINCIPLE #4
Strategic Questioning Techniques Help
You Discover Specific Answers

CLUE:

Don't Just Memorize Questions--Master the Concepts

"You're not finished when you've asked the right questions. Understanding and learning from the answers is what leads you to success."

Omar Periu

Whether questions are poorly worded and timed or well-thought-out and carefully-worded, they provide what no other selling strategy does—information. Successful investigators know that poorly-asked or -timed questions hinder your chances for positive sales results. Failure to master the power of the proper questions will limit your efforts to amateur status. Prospects will immediately identify you as a novice salesperson or a pushy dictator. If they believe you to be an amateur, they will either be hesitant to put their faith in your suggestions or they may try to take advantage of you. If they see you as a dictator, they'll turn off to your efforts and seek products to fulfill their needs elsewhere.

Good questions do nothing but strengthen your sales efforts. Well-thought-out and properly worded questions give you a polished, professional manner. They serve to convince your prospective customers to own your offering by building strong rapport and allowing them to discover for themselves just how your product or service will bring them the exact benefits they're looking for.

By practicing the quality questioning techniques presented in this chapter, and recognizing the negative results of the poor questioning strategies you may have been using in the past, you'll be on your way to becoming a top notch investigative salesperson.

What Do Good Questions Achieve?

1. *Good Questions Find the Answers When Building Rapport.*
   When you learn to ask questions in a warm and friendly investigative manner, your prospective customers will respond in the same way.
   - Good questions can establish common interests and help the prospect relate to you on a more personal level.
   - Great questions can actually put customers at ease and cause them to let down defenses they may have constructed to resist you and your offering.

When you enter the office of a prospective client for the first time, be the investigator. Now is the time to ask <u>yourself</u> some questions. Remember those observation skills!
   - What do the furnishings say about the customer?
   - What information can be gleaned from the items on his or her desk or walls?
   - Is there anything in sight that would indicate hobbies or personal interests?
   - What do displayed awards say about the position of power this person holds in the company?

A quick inner observation and mental questioning period before beginning conversation can provide you with excellent ways to build rapport. **Ex:** Even if you don't play tennis, you might ask: **"I couldn't help but notice your tennis trophy. How long have you been playing?"** Or, **"How did you become involved in tennis?"** The same could be said for a business trophy or an award of any kind. Ask the prospect questions about it. Most likely, he or she will enjoy the opportunity to share information about achievements. Otherwise, the trophy wouldn't be in an obvious location like an office. Make the prospect's accomplishments <u>your</u> focus when first entering his or her office.

2. *Good Questions Prevent Misleading Or Inaccurate Assumptions By Helping You Discover Clients' Needs and Wants.*
   One of the most irritating things a salesperson can do is assume they know what the prospect needs or wants. In fact, by asking well-prepared, well-worded questions, you can more quickly move on to a successful presentation. The true professional knows how to ask good questions, before

the meeting, so inaccurate assumptions are never formed in the first place. **Ex: "What special features do you wish you had on (your product or service)?"**

3. *Good Questions Find the Answers To Objections By Identifying Benefits!*
When you actively listen to the prospect's legitimate objections and ask relevant questions that help to dispel their concerns, you're on your way to a successful close that will benefit both you and your customer. Asking quality questions will maximize your offering's benefits to the customer and minimize his or her previously stated objection. **Ex: "Mr. Smith, I understand your concern. Would you like to have the purchase agreement reflect that concern as a condition of the sale?"**

4. *Good Questions Prevent Difficult Closings By Getting the Prospect Emotionally Involved.*
Good questions move the sale toward a positive close through gentle persuasion. The more effective your questioning techniques, the smoother the close. Sales is an emotional business; the better your questions create a picture of the prospect owning your offering, the more likely they are to own. **Ex: "Miss Jones, we take great pride in building our sparkling pools specially designed for a family like yours—one that loves to entertain on a hot summer's evening by taking a refreshing dip in the privacy of their own back yard. Can't you just picture floating in the pool, relaxing to the sounds of your boulder-crested waterfall?"**

Using questions is a great way to lead or direct the thought process of your prospect down the path of decision-making. There are four basic steps to leading with questions. They are:

Step #1:
Say something that makes obvious sense.
"Mr. and Mrs. Jones, research shows that a majority of Americans don't exercise and are out of shape."
Step #2:
Back up the fact with a personal story.

"I monitor the exercise habits of hundreds of people, and the biggest challenge I see with exercise programs is motivation."

Step #3:

Ask a question they'll most likely agree with that leads to the next step in your presentation.

"Would you agree with me that motivation is one of the biggest challenges facing people who really want to exercise, but just don't do it?"

Step #4:

Use a transition statement.

"Motivation is very important, and what I've found..."

You then move on to the next area of educating your prospects on how you can help them overcome the challenge they've just agreed they're having.

Poor Questioning Techniques Inhibit Successful Sales

1. *Poor Questions Can Eliminate the Customer's Desire to Own.*

    If questions are not worded to build a "yes" pattern, the constant "no" responses will eliminate the prospect's desire to own your offering. If the timing is wrong and the question is worded too strongly or argumentatively, your prospective customer will feel pressured and resist their first desire to own. If the entire questioning process isn't done with respect and concern and, instead, the focus is on how much money will be made from the sale, the customer's desire to give you any more time will be minimal. **Ex: What do you mean you can't afford my vacuum cleaner? You're living in a $250,000 home! I have to make a living too, you know!"**

2. *Poor Questions Limit Conversation Through One Word Responses.*

    If questions are worded so poorly that the expected response is one word when you're really wanting more information, the conversation will soon come to a dead stop. To continue these dull, go-nowhere conversations is pointless and makes everyone involved feel uncomfortable. Even if the response you get is a "yes" but it doesn't move you toward a successful sale, there has been little accomplished. **Ex: "Did you like the last copier you purchased from us?"** Wouldn't it have been more effective to say: **"What features did you like most about the last copier you owned?"**

3. *Poor Questions Diminish the Enthusiasm by Reinforcing Objections or Bringing Up New Issues Instead of Strengthening Needs.*
In most cases you are not clarifying the objection by restating it, you are simply strengthening or reinforcing it as a concern. Sometimes there are legitimate concerns that must be addressed. The majority of your time, however, should be spent discovering and strengthening the customer's needs instead of focusing on his or her objections. Enthusiasm is increased when the positive is fed. **Ex: "Can you imagine how much better you will sleep at night when you set that alarm and know that not one movement within three feet of the exterior of your home will go unnoticed?"**

4. *Poor Questions Prevent the Close by Pushing Rather Than Guiding the Customer.*
Well-designed questions gently guide the customer to a favorable response. The better questioning techniques you use before, during and after the presentation, the greater your chances of culminating the sale. If you get too over-anxious and pushy in your questioning strategies, you'll kill your chance to close before you've even begun. Listen to and watch your customers' verbal and non-verbal responses to your questions and let one question lead to another in a logical progression. Going for the close by asking pushy questions will get you a close alright—the close of the door on your backside as you're asked to leave. This is a matter of timing that's critical for you to master. Unfortunately, the most effective way to master it is through experience. Once you get the hang of the rest of the investigative principles in this book, you'll find mastery of this particular strategy almost a natural occurrence.

Ask With a Positive Attitude

Have you ever noticed how two salespeople can say exactly the same thing, perhaps ask the same question, and one will sound much more personal and caring than the other? Maybe it's the warmth in the salesperson's voice, the pat on the client's shoulder as the salesperson asks the question, or the smile on the face of a confident salesperson that makes the question sound totally different. Whatever professional salespeople add to the question, they do so with a respectful, positive attitude. They combine several techniques with their questioning that will soften or add enthusiasm to a probing or discovery question, such as: **"I'm curious, Mr.**

Jones, what computer are you using now?" Those types of questions get you the answers you need in order to prepare your case—your presentation.

When asking difficult questions, ones that great salespeople suspect customers will resist, salespeople often change the tone, pitch and speed of their speech. Their tone is one of confidence and understanding; the pitch is usually lower and the speed is somewhat slower. This creates less nervousness in customers because it smoothes out the questions, causing a less abrasive selling environment. It's kind of like the climax and ending of an action movie, the music builds or softens depending on what will happen next. The audience hears the intensification or relaxation, before they see it, through the emotional effects caused by the music. It's the same thing with good questioning strategies. Learn to build the excitement and emotional involvement in your product and service while, at the same time, reducing buying anxiety.

Like a curious investigator, an expert salesperson doesn't sweat a customer's aggressive question or stumble over it. Good salespeople know that what they have to offer is of benefit to the person they are presenting to, and the only way that customer will benefit is by first owning.

> It often takes nerve to ask those difficult questions the first time, but having the persistence to ask them the fourth and fifth time takes nerves of steel on the part of the determined salesperson.

However, nerves of steel, or at the very least a protective outer shell, are necessary if you're going to be any good at helping people make decisions and not take matters personally. It's kind of like a surgeon. A surgeon knows how to help the patient, but he or she also knows there's going to be some discomfort along the way. They learn to focus on the happy ending rather than the immediate discomfort.

More than that, it takes believing that you are doing your client a disservice if you don't persist and convince him or her to take you up on your offering. Practice asking those tougher questions with an attitude of dignity. Imagine that you have done business with this client for many years, and you know she would be disappointed if you didn't tell her about the wonderful opportunity she now has to join you in a business venture. You'd be surprised how contagious an enthusiastic attitude can be.

Create a "Yes" Pattern

Later in the chapter we'll talk about what type of questions to ask to create a "yes" pattern, but for now I want to establish the importance of building upon a number of "yeses" in your presentation.   When the customer is thinking "yes," no matter how insignificant the question, it's a good thing. In fact, it's just what you're after. The more "yeses" in your presentation, the more difficult it is to say "no" when it comes time to close.   One of the important things to remember is that this process should be completely natural, not over-acted and over-stressed. Learn to nod your head when you ask a "yes" question. Say "good" or "great" as you nod   your head.   Always give them a positive word after they give you a "yes". When you are positive and make others feel good about their answers, people will look to do business with you more than once. They wouldn't dream of doing business with anybody else.

Discover and Lead, Don't Aggressively Intrude

Your questions should naturally flow with the conversation. If you are firing a gazillion questions in rapid succession, never stopping to listen and respond naturally to the customer, you may gather a lot of information but it will be at the expense of building a trusting relationship.

That is my one major caution against any "tough-guy" image you may have of an investigator. You're not to grill your prospects as if they're the prime suspects in a major crime spree. You simply want to get them talking about the topic at hand, which happens to be their needs with regard to your product or service.

Six Steps to Building Rapport through Strong Questioning Strategies

When building rapport, the first thing to do is …

1. Care about people—ask caring questions. There's an old saying in business that "people don't care how much you know until they know how much you care." Take the time to investigate why people make decisions to own your product or service. When you do you'll be able to demonstrate that knowledge to your advantage with potential new clients by asking questions that target right in on their needs.

2. Strive to make your customers say "Me too" instead of "So what." Help them realize how much you really do understand their situation.

3. Demonstrate your product and service knowledge by refusing to start your conversations presenting benefits and features. Typical salespeople do this, not investigators. You begin your conversations with questions so you know exactly which benefits and features are most important to your prospects and don't waste their time with details that may not be important to them.

4. Ask questions that allow you to use a third-party testimonial. "Mr. Jones, with XYZ Corporation, had a similar situation and here's what he did. . ."

5. Be sensitive to customers' wants, needs and issues. If your product or service in any way involves sensitive or personal information such as people's financial, health or relationship matters, you'll need to adopt an even more concerned demeanor.

6. Keep in mind your customers will always be trying to avoid situations that they **feel** may hurt them and move toward selling situations that they **feel** will bring them benefits. People make judgments based on what they feel not on what they think. When asking questions, try to word them around what the customer feels, not thinks.

Omar's Famous 2 to 1 Ratio Recipe for Success

Whenever selling to a customer, keep in mind my 2 to 1 ratio. Ask two personal questions to one business-related one. This helps to alleviate any sales pressure and gets them linking positive feelings to their meeting with you because you're showing interest in them. During a follow-up meeting, remember some key words or topics you talked about beforehand. Bringing up past positive topics will help them feel those same positive feelings again and have good thoughts about what you're offering.

There is a very familiar rule that has been said in many different ways, but the simple truth is this: "Do unto others as you would have them do unto you!"

People will mirror your attitude, so ask questions respectfully and, guess what? They'll answer them respectfully.

If you ask questions with enthusiasm and caring, your clients will answer in the same manner. Make your customers the focus of your meeting. Ask questions that let them know your number one concern is their well being. It's much more difficult for prospects to say "no" to a salesperson with whom they've just spent an enjoyable 45 minutes of insightful and caring conversation.

Okay, I promised to teach you some questioning techniques that can be used to lead your customer to a successful close. Even though I want you to memorize these <u>types</u> of questions and recognize the best times to use them, you should be able to ask them comfortably and with your own particular attitude and style. No matter how well you know the right question to ask and practice asking it at just the right time, you'll get precious few positives in return if you stammer and bumble your way through it. Learn when to use the proper type of questions and then word the questions in your own easy manner.

STP Questions (<u>Seeking</u> <u>T</u>he <u>P</u>ositive)

You've probably heard of the tie-down, inverted tie-down and internal tie-down. They've been used so frequently that most savvy customers are aware of when you are using this technique, so beware! I call these my STP (*Seeking the Positive*) questions. These are the questions that continuously solicit positive responses, or "yeses" from the customer. Just like STP in the engine of your car gives it power and endurance—STP questions give your presentations those same benefits. They rev your selling engine and keep it running at peak "yes" performance throughout your presentation.

STP questions will begin with, end with, or contain somewhere in the middle, a request for agreement from the customer. The following are by no means all the tie-downs that can be used, but they will give you a start:

Isn't it?	Wouldn't it?	Haven't you?	Didn't you?
Doesn't it?	Shouldn't it?	Hasn't she?	Wouldn't you Agree?
Wasn't it?	Aren't they?	Isn't that right?	Won't you?

With these simple little "agree with me" phrases, you can change a statement into a question and before you know it your customer will be nodding in agreement and you'll be racking up the "yeses."

The best strategy for using this particular question type is to begin with a general question, which you absolutely know the answer will be "yes." You then follow that general question or idea with a need your customer has indicated, linking your offering to their need.

The following are some STP questions. See if you can easily identify the "Seeking the Positive" phrases.

Salesperson: "Didn't you say, John, that you and your wife have a five year old?"

John: "We sure do. He's a handful!"

Salesperson: "Let me show you a great feature on this new model refrigerator that was designed for families with young children. There is a small convenience door that can be opened and closed repeatedly without losing the cool air in the rest of your refrigerator. That would be quite economical, don't you think?"

John: "That would help. Billy is always fanning that refrigerator door."

Salesperson: "You've been looking for a long time for a refrigerator that would meet the needs of every member of the family, haven't you?"

John: "Yes, we've been looking for a while."

Salesperson: "Why don't you go ahead and authorize the agreement. Would delivery for the week day or weekend be better for you?"

John: "Will it be delivered before 2:00 p.m. on Saturday?"

Salesperson: "Would you like it to be delivered on or before that time?"

John: "Before that time would be even better."

Salesperson: "I'm sure that will be fine."

Once your customers' minds get used to working in one direction for minor issues, the "yes" direction, they will naturally follow with more "yeses" on the major decisions. Let me illustrate to you how one-tracked your mind can be. Join me in a little exercise that will show you exactly what I mean. Answer the following questions rather quickly and spontaneously, almost as if you were a customer answering what seemed to be rather insignificant questions:

• When you travel from one side of the country to another, what might you say you have done? You have traveled from _____ to _____.
  Answer: Coast to Coast.

• What is another word for the greatest number of something? A word that is more than the majority but a little less than 100 percent. **Answer: Most**

- What is a favorite meat your family may have for Sunday dinner?
  Answer: Roast
- What do you put in your toaster? **Answer: Bread**

If you answered "toast" or were at least tempted to do so, it was because your mind was on that track. You were like 99 percent of everyone who works through this little exercise. The same thing happens with those "yes" answers from your customers. Once they get on a roll, they are much more likely to keep up the positive responses until they own your offering.

 Like a good investigator, there are some visual clues you want to observe, as well. Before you go for more STP questions, you should look for non-verbal indications that the customer is with you. Leaning forward in their chair with an intent expression and a nodding head is a sign of agreement. It's now prime time to get a verbal positive from them.

A word of warning! Don't begin using STP questions until you have already asked discovery questions. It is only when you know what your customer wants and needs that you can follow up with STP's. If you fail to discover what the customer wants, your STP questions will not receive positive responses and, instead, you'll come across pushy and aggressive. Soon your selling engine will be backfiring! Another thing to remember is not to go for the big "yes" before you have earned many minor "yeses" by asking well-worded STP questions.

It's also important to know where to use STP phrases in your sentences. Let me give you some hints.

- Place them at the beginning of your sentences to sound warmer and more caring.
- Use them on the end of sentences for power or to gain control of that hesitant customer.
- Use them in the middle of a sentence so that they are not quite so obvious.

Sometimes you can even use them all by themselves as a stand-alone sentence to make strong agreement with a statement your clients just made. Don't you agree?

The Alternate of Choice Questions

In the last questioning technique we talked about how your mind will follow the path of least resistance and keep on track with that "yes" pattern. That's why you want to start a string of "yeses." In the beginning, it is much easier for most of us to say "no" than to say "yes". Why? Well, "no" requires nothing from us, and our customers feel the same way. "No" usually doesn't require money out of the customer's pocket. "No" usually doesn't require the customer to talk to their superiors about change. "No" rarely carries a heavy responsibility for the customer who puts himself or herself out on a limb, banking on the change being for the better.

Think about it. When you were last asked by a salesperson in a store the yes/no question "May I help you?" you probably said, "No, I'm just looking, thanks." What would your answer have been if that same salesperson had said "Would you like to see our new arrivals, or do the first-day sale items interest you more?" It's an Alternate of Choice question! Either way you answer, you are going to be looking at merchandise and that smart salesperson is going to be leading the way. This type of question gives your customers a choice to move forward, or advance the sale to a positive conclusion where everybody benefits. Now where is the bad choice here? Do you want your customer to move forward or advance? Now there's an Alternate of Choice question that's easy to answer!

Since timing, once again, is so important, let's discuss when to ask Alternate of Choice questions. The most common Alternate of Choice question is that which is used to get the appointment. **"Would Monday be a good day to meet, or is Tuesday better for you?"** Get the picture? Either way they answer, you've got the appointment. In our earlier example, we used one regarding the delivery of that refrigerator. "Would delivery for the week day or weekend be better for you?" Either way they answer, they've agreed to own the product.

The Ricochet Questions

I call the next type of questions my ricochet questions because I can illustrate the thought behind the strategy most effectively through this analogy. We all know what happens in the case of a ricochet. Something is shot or thrown. It hits its intended target, then bounces. It could bounce directly back or in a totally different direction, depending on the angle and density of what it hits.

You briefly dodge the initial question, but take advantage of the clue from it to investigate deeper. You have to be on your toes and recognize an opportunity to ask a question about a question. Here's an example. If your customer says "Does this copier come with a collator and stapler?" You

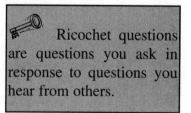

Ricochet questions are questions you ask in response to questions you hear from others.

would respond with: "Do you anticipate doing a lot of collating and stapling?" If you just answered their question with a "yes" or "no," you'd never learn the motive behind their question. Always seek out that motive.

If your prospect asks something you believe to be totally irrelevant to the investigative process, you'll want to ricochet back to the subject at hand with another question.

These types of questions make it possible for you to discover exactly what the customer wants when he or she asks you a question. The customer throws a question your way, and you throw another question right back that actually moves the selling situation forward and eliminates inaccurate assumptions made on your part that might hinder the sale.

The "COP" Question (Ownership)

COP stands for **C**onfirmation **O**f the **P**ositive. These are known as ownership questions. When the customer answers these questions, they have bought the product or service with their response. They are already seeing themselves as the owners of your offering. COP questions are used to get the customer emotionally involved with the offering or to confirm their emotional involvement. Look at the following example of a professional salesperson using COP questions to enable the customer to picture the ownership benefits while acting as though they have already agreed to own.

Realtor:	"Knowing you love that open floor plan, I just had to show you this home! Can't you just picture yourself curled up with a good book, reading in this room? Now this is the perfect example of that spacious, walk through plan you have been looking for, don't you think?"
Buyer:	"It sure is bright and open all right! And, it looks so big!"
Realtor:	"Did you notice how light that middle bedroom was with it's oversized windows?"
Buyer:	"Yes, I did. I'm thinking that would be the ideal place to have my home office."
Realtor:	"Absolutely! I guess there's no question where you'd put your desk, is there? Oh, and since you said you loved bird watching, wouldn't it be nice to have a bird feeder just outside the window of your office?"

Buyer:	"You were reading my mind."
	"Do you think I could fit my bookcases and files in here, too? I've never been able to have it all in the same room."
Realtor:	"Wouldn't it be great, then, to have them all in the same room? I believe you'd also be able to add on to your files and still have plenty of room to work. The previous owners' remodeling changes really helped. Without the closet you have a lot more room for more files, don't you think?"
Buyer:	"You know, we might even be able to fit a small working counter along that wall."

By using COP (Confirmation Of the Positive) questions, the buyers are now picturing themselves as the next owners of that home. They have mentally moved into that office. It won't take long for them to arrange their furniture in the other rooms as well.

The Know It All Questions (Sharp Angle Questions)

The Know It All questions or Sharp Angle questions are great tools to use after you have managed the conversation, allowing the customer to make a request that you <u>know</u> you can meet. "Know It All" questions are great closing questions. They are very effective because they seem simple on the surface; however, if used before you have built value into your product or yourself, you will come off much too aggressive.

When you ask these type of questions, make sure you know what you're talking about. Know it all about your company and or manager.

Once in a while those in shipping or upper management make exceptions to satisfy powerhouse clients to whom you have promised the moon. If you're a team player and don't make a habit of driving everyone around you crazy, your manager will support you on these special occasions. Let me give you an example of what I mean.

| **Prospect:** | "Can I get delivery by September 1st?" |
| **Salesperson:** | "If I can promise delivery before September 1, are you willing to authorize the agreement today?" |

The technique is really a simple ricochet question that asks for the sale.

Open-Ended Questions

 These types of questions direct the conversation. These are your who, what, where, when, why and how questions.

Open-ended questions are ones that require a more elaborate explanation from the customer. These have many advantages. One is that they give you a lot of qualified information. **Ex: "My research shows a trend in your industry toward more automation. How is your budget set up to handle the extra expenses this will require?" Or, "Who else will be on the committee to consider the purchase of the new office furniture?"**

Close-Ended Questions

Close-ended questions are easier to plan for, but can sometimes bring the conversation to a dead standstill. They are good when you are working with a limited amount of time, or plan for a "yes" or "no" in order to direct the conversation. **Ex: "Did you experience a great deal of employee turnover these past twelve months?"** These questions help you get a handle on which open-ended questions you'll need to ask in order to gather the information you need to help the prospect make a wise decision.

Solution Questions

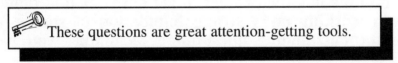 These questions are great attention-getting tools.

What could be more interesting than questions that lead to solutions that you can provide for the customers' situations? **Ex: "It was our experience when working with XYZ Corporation that their productivity increased by 20 percent when first implementing our quality control system. Do you have room for a 20 percent improvement in your productivity?"** This type of question is also called the "no-brainer" because it requires little or no thought to answer. They are excellent for opening doors for presentations and for closing sales.

Problem-Seeking Questions

> These questions specifically seek to uncover problems. They are more difficult to word than some of the other question types we've covered and oftentimes cannot be planned ahead of time.

This is where brainstorming before the meeting helps. More than likely, one of your colleagues or managers will anticipate a problem that you can plan to uncover through Problem Seeking questions. **Ex: "Your Facilities Manager informed me of a dissatisfaction with allotted space in the new factory. What spatial problems do you foresee within the first two years of production?"**

This chapter has given you a lot of information and many questioning techniques to practice, as well as specific times and circumstances to best utilize your newly acquired knowledge. It is up to you to investigate the impact these methods will have on your selling circumstances, and the best way to discover their effectiveness is to practice them. Don't let one or two unexpected negative responses kill your desire to keep questioning. It takes a while to get your timing down and your confidence up! There are few overnight sensations in the selling industry. It's a continual building process for long-lasting relationships between customers, yourself and your company.

There's no time like the present to get out your questioning tools and begin working on a strong foundation of successful sales through the outstanding questioning techniques you have just learned.

SUMMARY POINTS

- Good investigative questions…
  - ✓ Build rapport.
  - ✓ Discover customers' needs and wants.
  - ✓ Answer objections.
  - ✓ Get prospects emotionally involved.

- Poorly worded and timed questions…
  - ✓ Kill customers' desire to own.
  - ✓ Put a dead stop to conversation.
  - ✓ Reinforce and strengthen objections.
  - ✓ Push rather than pull the customer.

- Create a "yes" pattern through verbal and nonverbal communication.

- Six Steps to Building Rapport
  1. Genuinely care about people.
  2. Get customers thinking "Me too" instead of "So What."
  3. Don't talk benefits and features until you've established rapport.
  4. Use third-party testimonials.
  5. Find solutions.
  6. Give customers good feelings—take away fears through well-worded, well-timed questions.

INVESTIGATIVE PRINCIPLE #5
Investigative Selling is a Numbers Game

CLUE:

A True Investigator is also a Prospector

"Selling is finding the people to sell, and selling the people you find."

Tom Hopkins

What Is Prospecting?

Prospecting is what salespeople do to generate business, finding people who will benefit from their products and services and then convincing them to own. Prospecting is building your business by calling on people. It's also using effective marketing strategies and proven techniques to create warm prospects, and that's what you'll be learning about in this chapter.

Prospecting is not just for new salespeople with a little experience and a lot of energy, but for all salespeople who want to keep their production at an optimal level. You must first understand and expect that with prospecting there is a lot of rejection. Know this, though, your sales will go up in proportion to how many times you can handle your prospects putting you down and still stay up!

I know that may sound rough, like I'm asking you to take a beating. Not so! What I'm really asking you to do is refuse to take rejection personally. That is when you'll learn what top producers discover early in their careers—good prospectors have to learn to take the bad with the good. Now you know one thing about prospecting, it isn't always easy! I'll give you the tools in this chapter to become a great prospector, however, and show you how to make it fun. Make it fun? This may sound a little "out there" to you if you've already developed a fear of prospecting, but once you've seen how practicing effective prospecting can double and triple your income, you may even learn to love it? Trust me.

Adopt the Prospecting Spirit and Attitude

Because I hated prospecting so much early in my sales career, I refused to devote the amount of time to it that creates the numbers you need to be a successful salesperson. If that wasn't bad enough, half of my precious little prospecting time was wasted on the negative. I simply didn't have a positive prospecting spirit. Whenever I would come into contact with a prospective customer, I'd begin the conversation with apologetic language. **"Mr. Customer, my name is Omar Periu, and I hope I'm not bothering you this evening, but…"** Then it would get worse! If the customer actually assured me he had the time to talk to me, I'd press the point by saying **"Are you sure, now, that I'm not bothering you? I would be happy to call you back tomorrow night."** By this time, even the most patient prospect would begin to get aggravated at my lack of confidence. They soon began to agree that they had better things to do than listen to a salesperson who had no faith in himself or his product's ability to satisfy their needs.

Let me share with you a story that Dick Gardner once told me that changed my attitude towards prospecting, forever. It gave me that prospecting spirit. One time there was this salesperson traveling from one town to the other on a sunny afternoon to make his next meeting before the end of the day. There he was on this lonely road, miles outside of the city, when he heard a loud sound and his car began to dangerously swerve off the road. Bad news! Just as he suspected—flat tire. After thirty minutes of labor, he finally wiped his brow, put away his tools and was ready to hit the road again when suddenly he noticed something shiny a short distance from his car. He decided to investigate, and as he moved closer, he also noticed freshly turned soil piled around the shiny object.

Having the curious mind of most salespeople, the gentleman decided to investigate even further. As he raked through the soil with his fingers, he uncovered a large brick of pure gold. GOLD! He was so amazed that the gold brick fell from his hands, clanking against another gold brick buried just beneath it. Unbelievable! MORE GOLD! The more the salesperson dug, the more gold bricks he discovered.

The digging continued until the salesperson filled his car so full of gold bricks that it couldn't move faster than a crawl. But still more gold bricks appeared. He looked in both directions along the deserted highway, and just down the hill was a phone provided for travelers with an emergency. What do you think this salesperson did? He called his best friend in town and offered him an opportunity to become rich. In doing so, they would both benefit.

Think for a second! What would that salesperson sound like when he called his best friend? If you were the salesperson, how would you call your best friend to tell about the GOLD you had discovered? Would you be apologizing for bothering your best friend on a busy Monday morning? Would you offer to call him back later? **"Oh Mac, I hope I'm not interrupting you because if I am I can call back at another time. Are you sure, now? I know how busy Monday's can be. Okay! Well, I have discovered something in which I think, maybe, you might be interested. If not, it won't hurt my feelings or anything. So—-"** NO WAY! That's GOLD you're offering! Why should you apologize for offering GOLD to your best friend?

When it's GOLD, you should be grabbing that phone and dialing as fast as your fingers would allow. You'd be presenting that golden opportunity with so much enthusiasm and excitement that your best friend couldn't wait to participate in your adventure. And, if that friend foolishly decided to pass on the opportunity, would you give up? ABSOLUTELY NOT! You'd be talking to another close friend as quickly as it would take you to dial the next number. No apologies, instead you would sound something like this: **"You're not going to believe what I've just found. It's GOLD! Get a pickup, borrow a van, do whatever it takes, but get here, NOW! It's GOLD!"**

> The question you've got to ask yourself is, "Do you believe you have GOLD?" Are you letting other people know about it?

If you don't believe what you are offering is an incredible opportunity for your prospects, you're either representing the wrong product, providing the wrong service, or trying to convince the wrong prospects. When you believe in yourself and your product and service, you have to call on customers until you find those who feel the same way as you do about the opportunity you're presenting. You're offering a golden opportunity, and you know it is just a matter of time before finding others who agree with you.

After you make the sale, follow-up and service the account to identify additional customer needs and become their trusted problem-solver. When they trust you, they'll become repeat customers and tell others about you who will also become good prospects for you. You be the one to prospect; appeal to them, challenge them, answer their questions and concerns, develop their business and they'll turn to you every time.

Prospecting Is A Numbers Game—Top Producer Status Is the Prize!

Nobody plays the numbers better than the superstar salesperson. Most salespeople worth their salt know they must prospect. If they could only love to prospect, they'd become shoe-ins for sales success. It's prospecting that keeps most people out of the sales profession all together. It's lack of prospecting that makes most potential top producers throw in the towel. Why? Simple! They haven't learned to play the numbers game.

Prospecting is a consistent and methodical search for clients. Truly professional prospectors play to win. They're planning new prospecting strategies and practicing new scripts when others are winging it and wondering at their "bad luck!"

Effective Prospectors Are Not Born, They Are Self-Made

Let's investigate what makes the difference between poor, average and exceptional prospecting.

- ✔ Poor prospectors sit in the office wondering when the next hot lead will walk through the door, or they just sit there waiting for the phone to ring.
- ✔ Average prospectors will make a few calls, get a few rejections then quit for the day.
- ✔ Exceptional investigative prospectors will keep searching until they find just the right prospect.

They will ask questions of existing clients to find out what they enjoy most about their product or service, then seek out others who could enjoy those same benefits.

It's Not Who You Prospect, but How You Prospect

When I first started prospecting, I would set unbelievable goals with very little reward. I couldn't get into picking up the phone to "warm" call because there just wasn't enough built-in incentive to make me do what I had convinced myself I was just no good at doing. It was really my bull-headed determination to succeed and hunger for more in my life that made me prospect when my rate of success was about the same as Wimpy bargaining for a burger. In case Wimpy is before your time, he was the local deal-maker in the Popeye cartoons. Wimpy never had

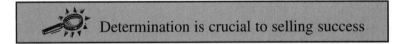
the money or smarts to get the hamburger he so desired, but he did have one thing that most salespeople could use a little more of in their selling careers. He had determination. He never quit.

> Determination is crucial to selling success

I knew if I was going to succeed in the area of prospecting, it was going to require a lot of preparation and perfect practice, and that it did. Let's look at these two things—preparation and perfect practice, and apply them one at a time as they relate to developing outstanding prospecting skills.

Before You Jump Right In, Coat Yourself with Layers of Positive Protection

Before you prepare materials and study salespeople who are master prospectors, you first have to prepare yourself, mentally. I could give you the old concepts about how there is power in the positive and how maintaining a positive attitude is one of the keys to success, but haven't you heard all that before? How do you stay positive when everything in your selling career is getting you down? You prepare yourself! Let me give you a few tips on how to do that.

 You need to layer your positive attitude, just like clothing, for the worst winter storm you've ever experienced. As you master a few more selling skills, you can peel off a layer or two and loosen up a little. You can get comfortable with your own abilities and warm up to your prospective customers. So, the following layers are what you should arm yourself with in order to remain positive:

1. The first layer should be those things that keep your energy level high. Make sure you exercise, eat a well-balanced diet and sleep well.
2. Over that energy layer, protect yourself with a coating of knowledge. Know your craft; identify your strengths and weaknesses; understand what has brought other top producers their success and do the same thing.
3. Next comes the protective layer of others. Surround yourself with professional, positive people who will encourage you to pursue your dreams. Then believe in them and in yourself and know that you will accomplish those dreams and they will support your efforts.

4. To stay really well protected, make that last layer one of almost unreasonable, never-ending enthusiasm. Look forward to the newness of each day, to its challenges and rewards.
5. Lastly, carry a shield of unwavering belief in yourself, a desire to succeed that is one-hundred times stronger than your fear of failure. When you do these things you can't help but be successful, and there's nothing like success to keep you positive.

Doing all these things doesn't necessarily guarantee a positive attitude all the time, but it will certainly take you a long way toward 'positive' when you are tempted to give up or give in.

When can you call it quits? Never! Not even when your nose bleeds from those slammed doors. Not even when the last person to walk through your front doors at the store is a family with ten, out-of-control kids running wild through your establishment.

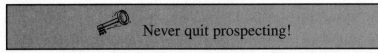

Never quit prospecting!

If they don't buy, ask them if they have any friends with a dozen adorable kids just like theirs who would be in need of your type of product or service. Now that's the difference between great and average salespeople.

Play the Numbers Game with Prospecting—and Win
One of the first things you have to do if you are to endure hours of prospecting is to set aside your emotions and adopt a good sense of humor. If you can laugh at your twisted words and not get hung up on feeling inferior, you come off looking confident and self-assured.

Remember, people don't always know when you've messed up. They are really saying "no" to your offering and not to you personally.

Learn to laugh things off. I do this by playing the "Bean Head" game. It goes something like this:

I used to keep some beans in my right pant's pocket when I knew I would be doing a lot of prospecting. When a prospect was particularly tough or even rude, and I was tempted to let their behavior pull me down, I quickly changed my attitude. I would say to myself, "You bean head, don't take things so personally. For some reason, calling myself that silly "bean head" name would bring a smile to my lips. Then, I would put my hand in my right side pocket, pull out a bean and switch it to my left pant's pocket. Before I knew it, I was able to move on to the next prospect with a fresh new start. No hard feelings—no left over negative attitude. As I'd feel the beans begin to fill my left pant's pocket, I'd know I was playing and winning the numbers game. I could do it ten times a day and nobody was the wiser.

Tom Hopkins used to put twenty business cards in his pocket every morning. He wouldn't let himself go home for the day until he had met and given his card to at least twenty people. You see, when you make a game of it, it doesn't seem so much like work, and you'll be able to visualize the outcome—twenty more people you've met today.

Reward Yourself for the Small Victories

It's like the game of Monopoly. Every time you pass "GO," you get $200. A sale may seem too far away and, perhaps, out of reach; whereas, making twenty warm calls in a day would be a major achievement.

Let me share a secret with you—if you set activity goals as well as end-result goals, you are much more likely to experience success.

In other words, whether your calls resulted in appointments, hang-ups or positive "come right overs," celebrate the fact that you made them. You stepped outside your comfort zone and did what it took to be successful.

Stay in that investigator's role. It is much more pleasant speaking with someone whose voice and mannerisms convey an easy confidence that comes from the natural approach. When you are asking for the appointment, smile. Your voice will sound like it's coming from a smiling face and generate enthusiasm. If you can't have fun, and at first fun may be out of the question, at least sound like you're having fun. You may even choose to practice in front of a mirror and record some of your calls in order to study your progress.

It's also possible to evaluate your performances through the revelations of video cameras and tape recorders. What an eye-opener that can be! You'll be amazed at how fast you speak when you're nervous. Most people listen to the tone of their voices on audio or video tape recordings and say it doesn't sound like them, when their friends say just the opposite. Sometimes it isn't what you say, but how you say it. Remember in Chapter Three when I told you that Dick Gardner, one of the great motivational sales trainers, once told me that it did not matter what I said on the phone because my enthusiasm was so great it was deafening? You can exhibit that same enthusiasm. When you've worked through this prospecting chapter, I want your enthusiasm by phone or in person to be at an all time high.

With Whom Do You Play the Prospecting Game?

If you are friendly and trustworthy when you prospect, building rapport right from that first contact, customers are much more willing to play the game with you. The fact is, prospective customers are looking for quality salespeople with whom to build relationships.

Prospects buy from friends before they do strangers—so be a friend.

One of my students said that her first goal in selling was to make 100 new friends a month and build all of them into strong business relationships. She did that in a short period of time and was well on her way to making a million dollars in annual sales. Her goal not only enriched her pocketbook, but her personal life as well. She learned, first hand, that when you sincerely want to help others, you don't have to worry about the money—it just flows!

It's Much Easier To Play the Numbers Game In Prospecting When You Know Your Success Ratios

The average salesperson thinks if he or she works hard enough, success will eventually come. That may be true; hard work is certainly a necessity. However, he or she may be working too hard prospecting where they are least successful and most frustrated. My suggestion is this: take two weeks and track your performance. Don't change what you have been doing; just go about business as usual. Then, change one little thing such as your opening line for the next two weeks and see if your ratios improve. If they do improve, keep using that new line and change another aspect of your prospecting method and track yourself again.

When I learned proper prospecting techniques, my sales took off like a rocket. Lift off wasn't the difficulty, maintaining altitude was the real problem. After my first year, I fell into a slump. It was a good thing I kept accurate records. I had concrete proof of what had worked before. I found that I had become complacent in my cold-calling, which lowered my number of contacts and in turn significantly affected my closed sales ratio. I've made it easy for you to track your sales activities as well by providing the following tracking form. Make copies and use one per day for the following two weeks.

ACTIVITY TRACKING FORM

Date	Activity	Results	Follow-up	Comments
7:00				
7:30				
8:00				
8:30				
9:00				
9:30				
10:00				
10:30				
11:00				
11:30				
12:00				
12:30				
1:00				
1:30				
2:00				
2:30				
3:00				
3:30				
4:00				
4:30				
5:00				
5:30				
6:00				
6:30				
Total hrs.				

The purpose of doing this exercise is to figure out a tailor-made numbers game most successful for your type of prospecting.

> By using the tracking form accurately and effectively, you will not only be able to calculate your sales ratios, but you'll also be able to see daily and weekly production patterns.

You will finally be able to put a dollar value to the "no's" you receive, making it much easier to swallow when you realize that a "no" answer just made you money and brought you one step closer to getting a "Yes!" Take a look at the following scenario:

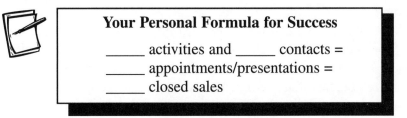

Your Personal Formula for Success

_____ activities and _____ contacts =
_____ appointments/presentations =
_____ closed sales

Let's fill in some of the above numbers to give you an idea of how the numbers work for you in prospecting. Everybody's numbers are different. For example, let's say that by examining your activity tracking forms over the past two weeks you realize that it took you 100 calls and/or contacts over an eight-hour period to make contact with 40 decision-makers. Of those 40 decision-makers you make 10 appointments. Of those 10 appointments you make 4 successful sales. Now you know your numbers and the average time it will take you to become successful. Under average circumstances, you must spend 8 hours prospecting 100 people to make 4 sales. Now let's reverse the numbers. If your goal is to make 10 sales a week, you must talk to 250 people and spend approximately 20 hours prospecting.

The Buck Stops Here

The thing I really love about sales is that I am directly responsible for my own income. If I want a raise, I don't have to worm my way into the boss' office and plead for a raise. I don't have to wait six months to a year, only to be forced to repeat the same process all over again. The best part is that I don't have to be disappointed when I work so hard and my merits are rewarded with a small token of what I really deserve, a pat on the back and a promise of more to come in the future. That's the beauty of sales.

Once you know the numbers, learn the materials in this book and know your personal sales ratios, if you want a raise you can do one of two things. You can make more contacts; thereby, selling more products or services. Or your other option is to work smarter instead of harder, and improve your sales ratios. I propose the latter. After all, there are only so many hours in a day and so many contacts you can make within that time frame.

Everybody Works Under the Same Time Limitations

Since I study successful salespeople and other trainers, I am always soaking up information that will improve sales strategies. I once heard my friend, Zig Ziglar, make a comparison between extremely successful salespeople and the average "Joe" beating the streets for each painful sale. Mr. Ziglar pointed out how much these two types of salespeople really have in common. Through his story, he emphasized the fact that average and excellent salespeople both work within the same time limitations. So, why is it that one salesperson is able to achieve so much more than the other? It really isn't all that difficult to figure out if you know your sales ratio patterns and the fundamentals of selling.

- The highly successful salesperson has learned to make the most of each moment and perform each day at peak level.
- The great prospectors have learned what methods pay them the most and what time of day it is most productive to use those particular methods.
- Successful salespeople also know when to do paperwork and return calls so as not to cut major inroads into their most productive prospecting time.
- Super-achievers have learned to be masters at time and territorial management.

Let's take a closer look at how to effectively manage your prospecting time.

Five Steps to Effective Time Management That Provide More Time for Prospecting

You'll do more in less time with much less energy expended by following these easy steps to effective time management.

1. *Keep a daily record of your time.*
   Make sure you use every moment productively, and don't get stuck behind your desk with no direction for your next few hours. You don't earn from behind your desk.

2. *Arrange activities into blocks of time.*
   By repeating the same blocks of activities each day, you get more comfortable and confident, and the repetition gives you higher returns for your time investment.

3. *Delegate.*
   By assigning less important tasks to others when possible, you have more time to plan, prospect and follow-up.

4. *Identify time wasters.*
   Whatever it is that is robbing you of precious prospecting time, identify and manage it. This may be one of your most difficult tasks in scheduling your time. You may find that time wasters are friendly phone calls and family chats during the day. Don't get rid of them all together, merely schedule a few moments each day that you allow yourself a chat with friends or family members. When that time is gone, it's back to the numbers game.

5. *Align your goals to your allocated time.*
   How much do you want to earn doing what? How much time have you allocated in each day to achieve your goals?

Okay, You've Prepared to Prospect—So Where Are All the People?

Wouldn't it be nice if prospects came packaged and delivered to your doors every morning ready to hear your offering? It probably would, but if it were that easy, everyone would want to be in sales. Believe it or not, I think if prospects were simply handed to me on a silver platter, I would become bored with selling. I would miss the challenge. Me, who hated prospecting, now saying this! How can you get to this point, too? Remember the game?

> Make it a point to be a student of sales and love learning. The more successful you are, the more you'll like what you are doing!

If you have specific territories to prospect, your time-management and organizational challenges can be a bit more extensive. Prospecting your territory takes, advanced planning, advanced appointment confirmation and clear communications of customer needs, especially if your assigned territory is hundreds of miles from home. Although today's technology has made our world a smaller place, prospecting in a large territory is usually more expensive. It also requires more time-management, better organizational skills and a more thorough follow-up system that lets you know that things are being taken care of even when you aren't there to personally oversee them.

New In Sales? Prospect the People You Already Know

The first thing you need to do is have a healthy list of prospects. For most, the first resource is their sphere of influence—their family, close friends and acquaintances. If you haven't already done so, make a list of at least 100 people you know. Don't qualify or prejudge the names on the list, just write them down. Refuse to stop until you have at least 100 names on your sphere of influence list.

For those of you who are stuck at 20 and think that it will take you longer to list 100 names than your pocketbook or life span will allow, let me make a few suggestions that could add to the list.

1. Family and friends first.
2. Do you have any hobbies?
3. Who do you know who enjoys the same hobbies?
4. Maybe you golf with a foursome or play bridge with a group of card lovers.
5. Some of your most successful prospecting attempts will be with those prospects who have a lot in common with you.

Okay, that should have produced a few more names. Remember not to prejudge or categorize yet, just list!

Actually, as a salesperson who prejudges people or situations, you may be negatively affecting your chances for greater income possibilities.

Let me share a short story with you about the time some salespeople misjudged me when I bought my first brand new car.

I was about 22 years old and very excited about purchasing a little MGB. I had received a personal loan and arrived at the car dealership with $7,900 cash in my pocket. I cruised into the showroom in my 22-year-old attire, t-shirt and jeans, and patiently waited for a salesperson to write up the paperwork so I could leave with my car. The sale was what we in the business call a "lay-down." I needed no convincing. I wanted that red convertible beauty in the showroom, and I had the money to buy.

As it turned out, many salespeople passed by as they went outside to join their buddies in a smoke, but none asked me if they could help. They probably took one look at me and decided I was just a kid looking to spend an early evening test driving sports cars that I'd never be able to afford, so they discounted my seriousness. Finally a woman salesperson approached me and was smart enough not to prejudge my ability to purchase. After just a few questions and about an hour finalizing the paperwork, I was leaving the parking lot with the top down to my new sports car, the wind blowing in my hair and a huge smile on my face. I couldn't resist passing by all those salespeople smoking outside and smugly calling out "Lay-down boys! This was a lay-down!" They missed an easy sale because they made an inaccurate judgement.

Okay, enough about prejudging, now let's get back to forming the list. Take a look at your community and religious affiliations. Do you go to church? Who goes there with you? Do you belong to an auto club or a computer club? Who are the other members? More names? Not bad—you're getting there. Now, are you a parent? If so, who are the friends of your children? What about their parents? Who teaches your children—school teachers, music teachers, scout leaders, etcetera? What about your professional sphere? Who are your doctors, dentists, attorneys, counselors? What about sports? Do you have season tickets that seat you next to the same people every week? Who are they? Get the picture? Statistics show that the average person comes into contact with hundreds and thousands of people. We just have to be reminded of who they are. That should have given you a start. No, don't you dare give up at 80. Make a commitment to list at least 100 prospects.

Already in Sales? You Have the Advantage!
For those of you already in sales, you are definitely at an advantage when it comes to prospecting.

✔ You have current and past customers to prospect.
✔ You have referrals from satisfied customers.
✔ You have customers who haven't received proper follow-up from other salespeople and are in desperate need of your services.
✔ You have other salespeople in related fields with whom you can swap names.

And the prospecting leads just keep on coming. In fact, you know what? You do have an endless supply of prospects just waiting for you to contact them. Have you died and gone to prospecting heaven, or what? Let's break down each one of these prospecting sources just mentioned and learn how and when to approach them for the appointment and eventual sale.

Prospecting Your Current Customer Base

Next to your sphere of influence, your current customer base is usually where you will have the most success.

Think about it, they are already using your product and they like and trust you. They are more likely to return your calls and respond favorably to your offering if you have provided quality service. If you have been a good investigator, you already know much of their background, including their likes and dislikes. Use what you know!

You also know what their payment history is like, so you may be in a position to offer special financial arrangements enabling them to own your product or service, NOW. You can sell them a new company offering, upgraded features on the product they already own, or simply more of the same. You can sell them on additional service packages or greater purchasing power your company is now extending to its preferred customers. Even if you sell them on nothing but the appointment, all is not lost. You have kept them updated, serviced your existing accounts, and you can always ask for referrals. That's a whole other category, isn't it?

What About Those Referrals?

This is one of the most neglected areas for novice salespeople. They don't take advantage of harvesting referrals. Why? They just don't ask for them. If they do ask for referrals, the standard question goes something like this: "Do you know of anyone who might benefit by owning my product or service?" Your first mistake was asking a yes or no question. In most cases when you ask a yes or no question, the answer is going to be "No!" It's less hassle for the customer to simply answer "no" and leave it at that.

> It's the job of a professional salesperson to make the customer feel good about offering referrals and, in fact, become a constant source of referral business.

Look at the following script on asking for referrals, and let's investigate some of the positive selling techniques used to build a strong referral base. It's a five-step process!

Example:

Salesperson:	"I really appreciate your time today, John, and want to congratulate you on owning our top of of the line computer system. Let me ask you, who is the first person you're going to show your new computer to?" (STEP ONE: Focus in on names and faces.)
John:	"I can't wait to show my neighbor, Tom, and have him take a look at it. In fact, he might be able to give me a few hints on how to run this software I just bought."
Salesperson:	"John, may I ask you another question? When Tom is in the market for a new computer, would you like him to be served by a company you know makes a superior product and a person you trust to provide quality service?"
John:	"Well, sure. But, I'm not sure Tom is able to buy a new computer system at this point. He and his wife are expecting a child soon."
Salesperson:	"Yes, having a child can sure make extra demands on both your pocketbook and your time, can't it?"
John:	"Sure can!"
Salesperson:	"And, that's why, John, I would like to be there for Tom when he is in the market for a new computer system. Even if it isn't this year, he'll know who to go to when he needs information and convenient financial arrangements

	just like what I was able to do for you. Since I want to be sensitive to Tom's needs, when do you think would be the best time to call?" (STEP TWO: Ask a qualifying question.)
John:	"He's usually out working in the yard on the weekends; I'm sure I'll see him on Saturday."
Salesperson:	"Great! I'll deliver the additional software that comes with this unit on Saturday, and perhaps you wouldn't mind introducing me to him while I'm out this way." (STEP FOUR: Ask for an introduction.)
John:	"Sure. That would be fine!"
Salesperson:	"How do you spell Tom's last name, John? Good! Just in case I miss you, what is a number where I can reach Tom at his convenience? If you should be out, may I say you gave me his name and thought he might like some information on our computers?" (STEP THREE: Ask for phone number. STEP FIVE: Ask if you can use their name.)
John:	"It's okay to tell Tom I sent you."
Salesperson:	"I appreciate your help, John. And, when Tom is in the position where he is needing a computer, he'll thank you for your consideration as well. Let me know if there is anything you need before I come out on Saturday."

You'll notice, it took a little persistence on the part of the salesperson, but he or she was determined to get the referral. You don't have to be pushy, just persistent.

> You can maintain a friendly attitude and position of wanting to help when you ask for the referral. If you never ask—you'll never get!

Let's review the steps to getting the referrals. After you read through them again, go back through the above dialogue and make sure you recognize them. You'll realize that they don't necessarily have to be asked in the same order, but make sure you don't give up on getting that referral until you've at least tried all five steps.

> **Five Steps for Getting Referrals**
> 1. Focus in on names and faces.
> 2. Ask a qualifying question.
> 3. Ask for address and phone number.
> 4. Ask the customer to call the person for you or to make an introduction.
> 5. If they resist, ask them if you can use their name, a testimonial letter or both.

Prospecting Past Clients Who Are Primed to Purchase

It's always better business and more effective to prospect past clients with whom you have established a successful service history. Keep in touch with them through mailings, phone calls and face-to-face check-ins. Let them know you value their business, and they'll let others know they value your product and being represented by a professional such as yourself.

Each product or service has a renewal history or length of time until the account matures.

> When you know your product and can identify the buying cycle of most of its consumers, you'll know the best time to approach them on owning a new model or an upgraded version of the one they currently own. This cycle is known as the "itch" cycle.

It takes some research, but don't be afraid to investigate your customer's itch.

Create the "Itch" Then Offer "Scratch" Relief

The great thing about the itch cycle is that you don't have to wait for the symptom in order to provide "scratch" relief. In fact, if your investigations show that most of the company's consumers buy again every 18 months, you'll want to start tickling that itch a month or two before your past client has realized his or her need to scratch. Professional salespeople create and reveal needs to past customers, and then guess who's there to address their needs? Their perception is that you serve them so well, you can anticipate their wants and needs at just the time they came to realize them.

Ongoing Scratching Service Produces Satisfied, Long-Term Customers

Calling on past customers shouldn't be a one-time thing when you need to make another sale at the time of their itch, though. It's a series of calls just to check up on how they are doing and how they like the product.

> Keeping in contact with past customers is a matter of developing a professional friendship based on honesty, integrity, and an attitude of helpful service. Many of these calls should be done face-to-face.
> - ✔ Get in the habit of dropping by just to help them out with any needs they have.
> - ✔ Let them know you are easy to reach and ready to serve.
> - ✔ Prepare them for the next sale by letting them know when new products come out or when improvements have been made to their current model.

Your enthusiasm and continued excitement will keep your past customers feeling the same way about you and your offering.

You know what, I don't even agree with the term "past clients." All your clients should be current ones if you are serving their needs on a continual basis. After all, they may have bought in the past but they are using in the present, right? If they are no longer using your product and you didn't know until you called on them during their itch cycle, you haven't been doing a great job of servicing that account, have you? There is another area where past customers come into play—they are the past customers of past salespeople in your company.

Prospect Past Customers of Past Salespeople in Your Company

Since salespeople are rather free-spirited individuals who value taking advantage of the best opportunities, they may occasionally move out of the area or change companies, advance up the corporate ladder or accept opportunities that move them into another product line or service. When this happens, they leave behind an entire database of customers. If the salesperson did a good job, there can be a gold mine of customers waiting to be prospected. If the salesperson did a poor job, your challenge may be a bit more difficult. However, with good communications and servicing, the opportunity will be there for you. All you have to do is ask.

Those who are respected by their peers are often approached to service accounts or territories that another leaves behind. Don't think your customers are the only ones to notice organized, well-planned business practices. Of course, your sales volume will reflect your hard work, but so will your testimonial letters and the praises of your peers.

> Treat your peers with the same courtesy and respect as you do your clients because they may, some day, fall into that same category.

Asking your sales manager for company files is also a good idea. If you are new to the company, you may want to practice some good investigative skills once again. First, learn about your product and its itch cycle. Then, with the permission of those in authority, look in files from that itch cycle time forward. Begin to make calls on clients who need scratching and have no in-house salesperson to remedy their itch. You'll be pleasantly surprised at the success of this type of prospecting.

Prospect Other Prospectors

Every sales industry has related sales industries teaming with ambitious salespeople much like yourself. Recognize the potential these affiliates have and you will have tapped another prospecting gold mine. Realtors have a good handle on the importance of prospecting other Realtors who represent the same types of properties. They form partnerships that are not company exclusive and alliances with Realtors they have enjoyed doing business with in the past. The operative word here is partnership.

Other industries should also be practicing what these Realtors® learned a long time ago.   Stop resenting your competitors for their success and begin investigating   what they are doing that you should be doing to improve your business.   Learn from other salespeople. You will find others have experienced the same things you may be going through right now, and they are usually more than happy to help. It never hurts to ask.

After having driven a BMW for many years, I was in the market for a different style or make of car. I went to my longtime BMW salesperson, Art, and told him how much I appreciated his years of service, but that I just didn't think I would be buying another BMW this year. Of course, Art attempted to change my mind, but when he understood I was simply wanting something different, he knew just what to do. He referred me to a friend of his, P.J., next door at the Mercedes dealership. Art and P.J. had been referring business for years, and each knew the other would treat their clients with respect, fairness and honesty. Art had once again satisfied his customer and still made a referral fee for his added service. Everybody benefited!

Now that we have talked about some of the places and people to prospect, let's talk about prospecting methods and strategies. There are as many different ways to prospect as there are people, but to help you out I have chosen three of the most common prospecting methods and given you helpful hints on how to prospect by using these methods.

1. Face-to-Face Prospecting

There are many ways to meet your prospects face-to-face. You can group prospect, network with other business executives or arrange the more intimate one-on-one meeting. Before you begin any of these methods, let me give you a few pointers.

> Write a 60-second personal commercial about your company and what you do that is of benefit to the client.

In doing so, when a prospect approaches, asking what you do, you can respond with a concise, interesting statement that focuses on their needs instead of your talents. For example, instead of saying: "I'm in public relations," you may want to say, "I'm an informant." Doesn't that sound interesting? When you've got their attention, continue with "I let every corporate executive with whom you would like to do business know exactly what it is you are offering. So, just what are you offering?"

Always reverse the conversation back to what they do. This is your time to let your investigative selling skills shine. Find out what they do, what position they hold, and what products and services they offer. If you are at a group gathering, make sure you pass on the information. Collect as many business cards as you do facts. As soon as you walk away, jot down a few things of interest on the back of the person's card—facts and information you have gathered. When you meet another whom you think would benefit from their service or product, introduce them to one another. They'll be impressed by your thoughtfulness and your thorough investigative skills.

If you are face-to-face with one individual, that 60-second personal commercial I mentioned before is also quite valuable. It lets you focus on them.

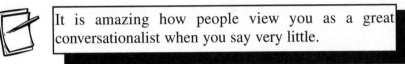

It is amazing how people view you as a great conversationalist when you say very little.

If you listen to them and make their needs the center of your conversation, they come away feeling important and valued. Meanwhile, you've made a great first impression.

2. Prospecting Over the Telephone

Although this is one of the most common forms of prospecting, it is also one of the most dreaded methods. It often requires a great deal of persistence to get through extremely efficient gatekeepers, somewhat protective secretaries, and voice mail messages to discover just who is responsible for making decisions pertaining to the purchase of your product or service. Persistence is one thing, but prospecting by phone and maintaining your enthusiasm and excitement while doing so can be a real challenge. You may have heard about putting a mirror by the phone while smiling and making sure your expression is warm and friendly when you talk to someone, but there's more to phone prospecting than meets the ear. Here are a few things to keep in mind if you're like most of us and much of your business is done over the phone:

- In most cases the purpose of the phone is not to close the sale, but to begin the selling process by getting an appointment. If that is the case, getting the appointment should be your major objective.

- The most common reason salespeople are rejected when attempting to schedule an appointment over the phone is because they are not the customers' first priority. Other reasons are that the customers are not in the frame of mind to talk about what the salespeople are offering; it is poor timing or they have no time to spare; or they just don't like your tone or attitude.

- It's much easier to say no to an offering on the phone. If your business allows it, make the phone your appointment partner not your negotiating ally.

Here are a few sample scripts that you may choose to reword a bit, internalize and make your own.

Example:

Prospect:	"Hello, Doris Hall speaking. How may I help you?"
Salesperson:	"Hello Ms. Hall, (never call them by their first name unless you have their permission to do so), this is Omar Periu, with Omar Periu International. How are you doing today?"
Prospect:	"I'm doing great."
Salesperson:	"Great! Ms. Hall, are you familiar with our company?"
Prospect:	Says "yes" or "no."
Salesperson:	In a few short words tell them who your company is and what they do. I'm talking about just a few sentences now. **Ex: "Our company is _____. We _____."**
Salesperson:	Now that you've identified yourself and your company, you need to qualify your prospect by saying something as simple as **"I'm calling to _____, and what I need to know from you is _____."**
Salesperson:	One of the most important steps to this process is to assume you have sold them on getting the appointment, with a sentence that goes something like this: **"When would it be convenient for me to drop by this week? Would Monday at 9:00 a.m. be good, or is 11:00 a.m. better for you?**

In call back situations, the following script will give you some ideas to build upon.

Salesperson:	"Hello Ms. Hall. This is Omar Periu with Omar Periu International. When we ended our call last week you asked me to give you a call back today to discuss setting up some training for your new home sales associates. Are there any questions I can answer for you about our services?"
Prospect:	"No, I think you've made your services very clear."
Salesperson:	"Good. I'll be in your area on Wednesday. Would 10:00

a.m. be a good time to drop by, or is 11:00 a.m. better for you?" Again, you've assumed the business.

If there are only two things you remember when prospecting by phone;

1. Don't prospect by phone in long, tedious stretches of time. Your attitude of boredom and frustration will soon be revealed in your voice. Prospect by phone for a while and then change methods.
2. Don't lock yourself into such a tight script that you sound mechanical. Use your body, your sense of humor and your creative spirit. Of course, you will always need to give them your name and company, but design that 60-second commercial with built-in questions that speak to the needs of the customer in a fun and exciting way.

3. Prospect By Mail

When you are prospecting by mail, your creativity is more important than ever. Sending a form letter that looks like a gazillion other form letters isn't going to get you far.

> To be memorable, you have to dare to be different.
> • Use your prospecting materials to tease your customers and excite their curiosity.
> • Avoid dropping off materials unless you know you have nothing to lose.

Maybe you've tried repeatedly for the appointment and haven't received a returned call. Perhaps your contact is out and won't be back in the office for days. Then you may consider leaving your material behind and make reference to setting up an appointment next week.

Provide just enough information about you and your company to give them an idea and a picture of your professional image, then leave them wanting more. It's like a great performance. Leave the stage when the audience in standing and calling for more.

Investigate your prospects' needs and appeal to those needs when you mail them information. If you know that they have recently merged with another firm and may be experiencing financial constraints, appeal to the economical aspects of your product or service. If you know that your prospect is looking to expand in another market, give them testimonials of customers you serve in their targeted markets or examples of how you have helped other companies through similar expansions. Results come from what you have to offer and how you present and deliver your offering.

Electronic Mail—A Whole New Venture in Prospecting
Electronic mail is quickly becoming one of the most efficient methods of direct mail in today's market. Think about it. When you e-mail the customer direct, you don't have to worry about getting past the gatekeeper or being lost among the hundreds of other communications atop your prospect's desk. It has been my experience that e-mail is given a higher priority. In most cases, the most difficult aspect of e-mail is discovering the prospect's e-mail address. It may surprise you to know that in many on-line services, getting a user's e-mail address is as simple as entering a membership directory and inputting their name, city and state.

Prospecting On the Internet
The Internet is a great method of prospecting for national accounts. The challenging part is that everybody and his brother has a web site. In addition, the Internet is crowded with a lot of meaningless data that you'll have to learn to wade through in order to connect with qualified prospects. If you are unfamiliar with the Internet, my suggestion would be to go to your local bookstore or library and discover the Internet world. A word of caution!

The Internet is a lot of fun and can be very distracting, so keep your prospecting purpose in mind when you browse the web. Learn to browse on your down time; do specific web prospecting during your selling time.

Prospecting Via Fax

Fax numbers are another form of easy and direct access to the client. I do need to caution you, though. There are some heavy government regulations regarding solicitation through electronic devices without the express permission of the client, so make sure you abide by the laws that protect one's privacy.

Don't Make Excuses—Make Contacts—Make Money

If you try hard enough, you can always find excuses that postpone prospecting. There are also many causes of procrastination. Many of you even think you have legitimate fears that inhibit your prospecting capabilities. I disagree. We are born with only two real fears: the fear of loud noises and the fear of falling. Unless you're prospecting cliff-side during a hurricane, you'd better rethink that fear factor. Don't take yourself so seriously; prospecting isn't a life or death matter. If you make a mistake, learn from it. If you stumble over your words, laugh. I can assure you, that is exactly what your prospect will want to do, so give them permission.

> Make a game out of prospecting and you'll be the winner every time.

Remember: prospecting is a numbers game. If you aren't out there contacting the numbers, you won't make the dollar figures you're counting on in your selling career. Keep in mind, sales superstars are made of the stuff that drives them to get up when rejection and negativity keep the average salesperson down. Their success is not based on how many times they fail, but on how many times they rise above the negative and turn those negatives into positive learning experiences.

Do What the Great Ones Do

Once again, you will want to find out what the sales greats are doing that has made and continues to make them the best of the best. Be an investigator; discover what they do that you can do even better, then do it. Be determined to be the best in your field, and don't feel guilty about out shining your mentors.

The best teachers want the best for their students. They're pulling for you, and so am I!

SUMMARY POINTS

- Make a game of prospecting; play by your rules with you as the winner.
- Self-disciplined, self-confident, self-motivated—these are the keys to successful prospecting.
- There are two ways to get a raise in selling:
  1. See more prospects
  2. Improve sales ratios by improving your selling skills.
- Have a sense of humor when you prospect; give you and your customers permission to laugh at your mistakes.
- Make your list of 100 possible prospects and work your list.
- Prospect on the Internet.
- Use the tracking forms to determine what prospecting methods and times work best for you.
- Using the formula, place a dollar value on your "nos."
- Where do you find all your prospects?

  - ✔ Sphere of influence
  - ✔ Library
  - ✔ Managers
  - ✔ Fellow salespeople
  - ✔ Sponsors within the company
  - ✔ Past clients
  - ✔ Current customers
  - ✔ Old company files
  - ✔ Referrals
  - ✔ Internet

- Write a 60-second commercial with built-in questions touting your strong points and the benefits you can offer your prospects.

INVESTIGATIVE PRINCIPLE #6
Make the Investigator's Connection--
Develop and Build Rapport

CLUE:

Build rapport first. Rapport levels the playing field and reduces the fear factor in your customer.

Trust Statement: *"I could work for any company, but I chose this one because of the quality of the products and services it represents and their high standards of customer service."*

Omar Periu

In the real world of selling, customers just don't want to be your friends, and you aren't too eager to be theirs, either. In many cases, the one and only thing that you have in common is that you will both benefit if the customer decides to own. In reality, it's not a personal relationship you're after at all but a business relationship that offers mutual benefits to both you and your customer.

There are still many selling situations, however, in which you can become good friends with your customers. They totally trust you to look out for their best interests, even when it means making personal sacrifices. Your number one motivation should be to satisfy their concerns and make sure they receive special treatment by your company.

> Customers who receive the best service you have to offer are yours forever, regardless of whether your competitors are currently cutting your price, offering additional features or delivering in less time.

It's more than just a mutually beneficial relationship; it's a mutually enjoyable friendship.

Wouldn't you like to feel that way about all your customers? You can. Have you ever experienced someone you don't know recognizing you and acting like they've known you for years? They approach you warmly, ask about your past, then what you're doing now. They may even ask about your plans for the future. Meanwhile, you're racking your brain to figure out how you know this person, acting friendly and cordial and answering all their questions politely. You're beginning to feel like this person really does know you. You feel singled out, special. Whether it's ever determined how you know each other doesn't matter. You leave the experience feeling good. It may have either made your day, or theirs.

It can be that way with your prospective customers as well. You can let them know that you are so genuinely happy to see them that they feel good when the meeting comes to an end. You'll enjoy your customers and your business much better if you treat every customer like they are special, and you value their business more than any other customer you have. You're showing interest; they're feeling valued! Great combination for building rapport.

> You can't afford to minimize the importance of prospective customers you feel have nothing in common with you. It's your responsibility to find something you have in common with them.

To do that, give them a chance to make that connection. Once again, I have to warn you that connecting with your prospective customers will be a near impossibility if you prejudge or practice poor communications with them. A master salesperson never prejudges a customer. You never know who you are talking to, so don't prejudge!

It's also necessary not to prejudge yourself and your abilities! When I took the plunge into learning to be a sales professional, I caught myself many times saying "I couldn't do that; that's too pushy," until a good friend of mine said, "Why not try it first? In our country you're innocent until proven guilty. In sales, you can until it's proven that you cannot. When I thought I just couldn't do that "pushy" stuff, no sooner would the thought pop into my head and there would follow such a challenge that I just had to prove myself wrong. I soon came to realize that it wasn't pushy to be determined to discover and fulfill a customer's needs. It wasn't pushy to follow up with them until I knew they were satisfied. It wasn't pushy to offer to serve the needs of their friends and relatives with the same level of concern I had for them.

Okay, what to do first? I did need the practice, but most of all I needed an attitude adjustment. I needed to learn not to prejudge others and myself. Why is this so important? Today, as a trainer, I realize that most salespeople don't have formal training and they have little time to read, listen to tapes or attend professional seminars. Since many were told they were born to be in sales because they had the "gift of gab," they spent their lives being average and shooting from the hip.

I consider myself proof positive that investing in your mind to develop strong sales skills makes a world of difference.

> You can have anything you want; you just have to be willing to sacrifice time and a reasonable amount of money to get it. You must be willing to pay the price!

What's This Rapport-Building All About, Anyway?

You've heard all this stuff about building rapport before, and perhaps you've even made a half-hearted attempt at small talk, but let me ask you a question. If you have to establish some kind of customer rapport because that's what all the sales gurus are telling you is necessary to go forth and prosper, why not give it your best effort? Who knows, you may have an outside chance of making a friend and some very strong business relationships to boot, just like the "100-new-friends-a-month" colleague I mentioned in Chapter Five.

When I first began my selling career, I did all the things that others said would help me build rapport, and, even if I must say so myself, I was better at it than most. Making conversation just seemed to come naturally for me. However, when I left the office after investing an hour of rather meaningless conversation, I felt pretty shallow inside. Finally, one day, I decided that if I had to do this rapport thing, I was going to give it the same enthusiasm and sincere effort that I gave to the rest of my selling career. I would make my next call one of interest in my customer, even if I had to dig deeper than ever before to find something in common. I planned sports discussions. I paid special attention to current events in the newspaper. I had laid the groundwork, and taken the first steps to rapport building that begin before the first meeting.

I discovered that my very next prospect, Ms. Fields, was a physical fitness nut who worked out as much as I did. Since I loved staying fit and discussing health and fitness issues, I knew that would be a great ice-breaker to making conversation that would earn me the right to spend time in her office. We'd get to know one another and I'd have a better chance of closing the sale. I was positive— pumped to go in and practice my best rapport-building techniques. So, I did just that . . . walked in, saw her body building trophies on the credenza, asked about the pictures of her family and friends, focused in on the fitness part once again, and we had a great conversation before the selling process ever began. The conversation was actually a very important part of the selling process. I was building rapport—building a relationship that would open the door to the selling opportunity.

Because we had so much in common, we did become friends and even trained together. Not only did I earn her bank branch as my account, but she also invited me to dinner with all the bank executives. I was able to put together a total corporate package that translated into a greatly elevated position for Ms. Fields and a significant income boost for me. With friendships like that, who wouldn't have a dynamic career?

Now That I Have Decided To Build Rapport, What Should I Do Next?

If you have prospected well, you'll already have the appointment and some idea of what your prospect is like. You can then initiate good conversation and be ready to enter the office with your eyes and ears open to rapport-building ideas.

Let's examine four short steps that will help you learn the rapport-building process. You'll find yourself at a great advantage if you remember these four steps when meeting face-to-face with your prospects.

Step One - Observe Your Surroundings

As you walk through the doorway of your prospect's office, enter with your eyes and ears open. Look at decorative colors, pictures, furnishings, seating arrangements, what's on the desk, and any indications of likes and hobbies that may be in the form of awards or trophies. Now observe your client.

- Is he or she married?
- Does this person have children?
- Does your prospective customer look athletic?

- What is their expression as you enter?
- During the meeting do they look contemplative, negative, rushed or preoccupied?

This first step in rapport-building involves asking yourself all these questions. Although it takes a while to run through these things on paper, it just takes a few moments when doing it in your head.

But, what about rapport-building in retail sales? It is often more difficult to build rapport in the middle of a busy sales floor with numerous distractions. You're not on their turf; they're on yours. That's when you'll need to be more observant of the customers themselves. Compliment them on their appearance or their good taste. In these situations, you can't be afraid to make it a little more personal, without overstepping your bounds, of course. **Ex: "What a beautiful family you have. You've done a great job parenting; your children are very well-behaved. How old are they?"**

Don't Forget

Remember, you have to thank them for giving you this time and show them how you're looking forward to serving their needs and wants. When customers trust you, they'll give you all the information you need to make a successful sale and return again and again.

Step Two - Ask Questions
Even though you've been asking questions all along to get them talking and build rapport, when you sense a better relationship forming, you'll want to direct the questioning for more pointed, planned results. If you need to, look back at Chapter Four on questioning techniques. Some of them will fit nicely during the rapport-building stage of the meeting. As your customer responds, you'll want to take notes and make observations.

Step Three - Take Notes
Okay, now that you've begun to collect a bit of information, like any good investigator, you've got to record it on paper. Pull out your notepad and, at the same time, ask your client if it's okay for you to jot down some notes. Most will have no objections. As soon as they give you permission, do one more important thing. Get out the pad of paper and all materials necessary to make the sale. When

you progress into your presentation, switch from taking notes on your scratch paper to making notes on your agreement. Before the end of the meeting, you'll have a good portion of your paperwork completed and your customer will be accustomed to watching you write. He or she will have less nervousness and more trust in you.

> Even if you don't make the sale that day, you'll have a lot of good information to study and bring to the next meeting. Those notes may prove invaluable at a later date, so don't throw them away if today's meeting isn't fruitful.

Step Four - Listen to Verbal and Nonverbal Language
This isn't really a last step; in fact, none of the steps go in any specific order. You'll be practicing first one and then another, then back to the first during the entire rapport- building process. Remember, you are building a relationship and those often take several meetings. Sometimes you'll immediately click with that person, and then again you'll find yourself struggling to make small talk with someone whose personality, likes and dislikes is much different from your own. When this happens, you haven't failed, you just need to work harder to adapt your presentation and personality to theirs.

> People like to own from people like themselves. So, match their rate of speech, tone of voice, body language, etcetera.

The bottom line is this: learn to be adaptable to different styles and different customers. Observe your customer's mood and adjust your behavior to ensure a comfortable selling environment. Observing another person's style of behavior will vastly improve your sales performance with almost all your contacts. So, what are the various styles? I thought you'd never ask!

Someone's Style Is More Than Just Mood; It's Predictable, Observable Behavior

What I learned throughout my selling relationships is to connect with customers on their terms, looking at things through their eyes, feeling the selling emotions through their experiences. That's when I began to take a "customer approach" to selling. What did I do? I became an investigative salesperson, and I put myself in the place of my customer so I could experience the selling situation from their perspective. I've said it before, but if you want to know how Tom and Mary buy, you have to put yourself in Tom and Mary's hide!

I do exactly what I've been telling you to do since Chapter One. I don't **tell**, I **ask**.

> I have stopped seeking to be the center of every conversation and search instead for clues to identify the real needs of the customers.

Along with hearing what is important, I observe behavior that shows me dominant character traits that make customers react to the situation and respond to me as they do.

The following are the three common behavioral types I have observed in most customers: visuals, auditors and kinesthetics. For each type, I've given you tips on what to look for to identify style, and how to best relate to that particular style. Once you discover the styles of your customers, successful selling becomes a simple matter of learning to monitor and adjust.

Visuals

Sixty percent of the population is focused on images. What they can see is what they value most. They relate to the world through pictures and visuals. You can determine those people who are visually-oriented by observing their eye movement. When pondering a thought, visuals will look up to the high left. The most common professions of visuals include graphic design, painting, photography and generally creative fields. You'll recognize them when they speak because they will use phrases such as "I see." or "Get the picture?" or "Do you see what I mean?" During presentations to visuals, you'll want to take advantage of your company's visual aids. If they are not bright and colorful, invest some time in color-coding or highlighting the most pertinent information. Take advantage of colorful and fast-moving computer presentations.

> Use graphs and charts rather than columns to show figures. Make your presentations eye-appealing.

Auditors

These types relate to the world through the way things sound. Their most common eye movement is to look from side-to-side and down. It's almost as if their eyes are helping their ears focus, attracting the information they want like a satellite dish. When looking down, they're, in essence, getting visual distractions out of their way. The most common professions for auditors include music, language, and communications fields. You'll "hear" them say things like this: "Tell me!" or "Listen to me." or "Can I tell you something?" or "I hear you." or "I hear what you are saying." With auditors, be especially careful with your words and enunciation. Put emotion into your presentation with your voice inflection and tone. Speak clearly and concisely.

> Allow them to make notes on what you are saying rather than providing them with a lot of reading material.

Kinesthetics

These types relate to the world through touching and feeling. Their most common eye movements are to look down and to the right. They are most often involved in "hands-on" professions such as teaching, nursing or other medical fields where touch is important. They like being involved with fabrics, agriculture or horticulture.

> Bring samples of your product to touch and feel. Hand them things to hold during your presentation. If you sell equipment, get them pushing buttons in order to engage their attention.

The Way to Be Heard Is to Listen

God gave us two ears and one mouth so we could listen twice as much as we talk! I'm sure you've heard this statement since you were knee-high to a grasshopper, but now it's time you listened and applied the principle to your sales career. If you really want to find out about prospective customers, it's time you tuned the rest of the world out and focused your direct attention on that one particular client you will be cloistered up with for the next hour or so. Sometimes silence is one of the better forms of communication.

When you are quiet, your client will usually take that opportunity to express himself or herself. Observe the behavior and listen to the words that offer clues about their style, and how your style can be adjusted to accommodate them.

Learn to read your customers.

✔ If they are as driven as you and can't wait to get on with things, you may find them more responsive to you when you move the conversation quickly and get to the point.

✔ If they are crunched for time, don't spend all afternoon chatting. Instead, just get down to business—they'll appreciate you for it.

✔ On the other hand, if an amiable person who loves to talk and is curious to know just who you are and what you are selling welcomes you, spend some additional time there. They'll want you to talk a little more about yourself and ask a few more social questions about them and their work.

✔ If you can, try to identify the customer's behavioral style before the meeting. Then you can plan your appointment accordingly.

It usually takes longer to accommodate the talkers than those who are driven to get you in and out and move on to other business.

 As a side note, if you have a prospect who insists on learning how much your product or service is before you've done a thorough investigation, use these words: "Mr. Garrett, no matter what I tell you right now, it's going to be too much because I haven't been able to show you the value of working with our company and using our fine products." This is a great way to put on the brakes and get back in control with a few questions that help you investigate their needs.

Mirroring the behavior of your customers is also a good idea. If customers talk fast and furious, pick up the pace of your speech. If they are more kicked back and like to think through their words before they voice them, don't interrupt them or finish their sentences. If their manner is rather formal, don't pull off your jacket and call them by their first name right after the initial handshake.

Caution: What you don't want to mirror is anger or frustration. If your customers are emotionally charged, remain calm and collected. If they are rather dry and boring, insert a little enthusiasm into the conversation and get them emotionally involved. Those are some pretty tall orders, aren't they? Not to worry, in time I know you'll do all of these things quite naturally.

There is one way that everybody wants to be treated. They want to be valued and given the opportunity to feel important. There is nothing like the appreciation and respect of others to encourage someone to open up more and return with a positive response. When you build rapport, you are really building your own business.

Besides Touchy-Feely Rapport-Building, There Are Proven Success Techniques That Can Significantly Increase Your Performance

I have already mentioned several success techniques in this chapter. One technique is actually the most underutilized task in planning for the call: researching the client and his or her company. More research may uncover just what area or branch of your targeted company could best use your products and services. Build such strong rapport that it is both inconvenient and next to impossible for your customers to be easily swayed by a competitor who would move in and steal the sale. Don't be cheated out of those big opportunities you've worked on for months by a competitor who may have better rapport-building skills than you. Investigate all your alternatives when building rapport. Allow your customer to feel as though they are leading the conversation. If you're not able to plan, always be ready to change. Be flexible and read the customer. Remember, customers will tell you how they want to be sold, so listen, listen, listen!

When Should You Begin To Build Rapport?

The process of building rapport should begin before you ever enter the office of your prospect. Rapport building starts in the planning stage. Research! Be thinking of ways to develop that relationship. When you speak to them on the phone, smile and match your voice with theirs and make them feel comfortable. Build rapport with others in the office as well as your client. It never hurts to have other contacts in the trenches.

Building rapport begins by knowing yourself and your own style. You will be unable to adjust your behavior to accommodate your clients if you don't know yourself and your style.

Building rapport could even begin with your customers' peers. After stating your objectives for the sales call with the CEO, his or her associate might offer additional information that promised to give you the leading edge. Before you meet with the customer, if you have learned that they enjoy a bit more conversation and you want to combine it with building rapport, you might want to plan out some questions you will ask. Consider mentioning some current events in the newspaper; just be careful to avoid controversial topics. The following is a list of taboos when talking to a customer:

1. <u>Don't Talk About Political Beliefs</u>
   - Everybody's got them but no two are alike.
   - Prospects might make judgments against you and your product based on whom you are voting for in the next election.
   - Politics is such a strong subject that it may distract you from moving into the sale.

2. <u>Don't tell—ask!</u>
   - Nobody likes a know-it-all. When you are building rapport, take your time and ask a lot of questions.
   - Save some questions for the qualifying process, but, for now, there's no time like rapport-building to venture out and practice your plan.

3. <u>Don't wear an expression of concern</u>
   - Smile and look them in the eyes.
     The first thing I ever noticed about the great motivational trainer, Zig Ziglar, was his smile. This man can energize a room. I've seen thousands of faces light up within moments of his appearing on stage with his great smile. In smaller settings, I've noticed Zig walk into a quiet room filled with strangers who may have been uncomfortable speaking to one another, and say, "Top of the morning to you. Isn't this a great day?" He's broken the ice. Before you know it, everyone in the room has something to say to the person next to them, even if it's "What a nice man he seems to be." Wherever Zig is, he is always happy to be there. I have to believe that his smile is one of the major reasons behind his past success in sales and current success in helping others through his training.

Use Precise Language and Pronunciation

Don't Forget

Remember, while you are observing your customers' behavior, they are doing the same to you. Make sure your language follows through with the image you have created for yourself. If your language makes you sound uneducated, do something about it. Learn to pronounce your words clearly and properly.

I had to do that with my accent. Because I came from a foreign country and was raised in a home where English was the second language, I had to educate myself to speak differently. As I studied to be a professional recording artist, my voice teacher taught me how to breathe and speak with clarity and feeling. I read Shakespeare's plays out loud for many hours. I practiced speaking and breathing so that I could hold a note and whisper an important line and still give it power and meaning. That's how I lost my accent, and how I gained the words and speaking habits that have made my career as a public speaker so successful. I was determined to be better, so I went the extra mile.

> If your speaking skills are substandard, it will be impossible for you to sell the company's CFO on the benefits of your product and service.

You'll never be able to convince them that you're the one they need to buy from in order to receive the best service. When you are talking sales, make sure your vocabulary is up to snuff and your written skills are above par.

Drop Names of Industries and Their Workers Who Have Benefited From Your Product

You need to be a little more cautious with this one because customers are getting a lot more sophisticated, and they could consider the "name dropping" to be a power play on your part.

> The key is to mention long-time customers in related fields that are currently using your products or services and have them readily available for references. Offer them testimonials in writing or over the phone so that they can speak directly to others who have benefited from your offering.

If you remember only one thing in this whole chapter, remember this: whatever your selling method, strategy or technique, don't lose yourself in the **telling**, find yourself enjoying the benefits of **asking**!

It's the Little Things that Can Make the Big Differences!

Take a few moments to say "thanks" or follow up with a customer when they've had a special award or achieved something worth recognizing. Not only will it make you and your customers feel good, but it can also get your foot firmly in the door during your next sales call. Here are a few suggestions you'll want to try the next time the occasion arises:

Follow-up Note After Presentation
Thank you for taking time out of your busy schedule to meet with me yesterday. I look forward to working with you and (company), and will follow up in the near future to see if you have any questions.

Follow-up Note After Purchase
Thank you for showing your confidence in me and (company name) by investing in one of our best products. I'm excited for you and look forward to serving your (product or service) needs in the future. I will stay in touch to make sure your experience with us is exceptional.

Follow-up Note After Referral
Thank you for your vote of confidence in me and (company name) for referring (name of referral) to me. I promise you, they will receive only the best service. Thanks again!

Follow-up Voice Mail
Hi (name)! I just wanted to leave a short message and thank you again for meeting with me. My goal as a (product) representative is to provide you with the most outstanding service possible. My direct line is (number). Please call me if I can be of further service.

Follow-up E-Mail
Hi (name)! One of the nicest aspects of cyberspace is that I'm only a few key strokes away. I check my messages three times a day, so please feel free to keep

me updated on how you are enjoying (product or service). I look forward to hearing from you.

Follow-up Industry Article
(Name), I saw this article in (publication) and thought you might be interested in it. My main goal is to keep you updated on new trends that will help your business. Please call me if I can be of help.

Follow-up After a Special Occasion
Congratulations on your (promotion, etc.)! I really appreciate your friendship and look forward to working with you in the future. Again, congratulations!

Follow-up With A Personal Gift
(Name), please accept this gift as my way of saying thank you for allowing me to offer you my company's finest service. I truly enjoy working with you and look forward to keeping you updated on (company name) new and exciting developments.

Follow-up After They Decline To Buy
(Name), thank you for your time in considering our (product or service). I understand our timing was off a little bit, but I look forward to serving you in the future. I will keep you updated on new products and services that will benefit you and your company. In the meantime, please don't hesitate to call if you have any questions.

Okay, this is the last thing I'll have to tell you about building rapport: say things three times. People don't hear the first two times. I said, "Say things three times. People don't hear the first two times." It's to your benefit and that of your customers to do what? Say things three times.

 Make sure that the last piece of information is memorable. Leave them with a good impression. Most of all, leave them with a promise to provide the best possible service, and you won't have to worry about starting the rapport process over again in your next meeting.

By practicing what you've learned in this chapter, your customers will soon be welcoming you back like the friend you've worked so hard to become!

SUMMARY POINTS

- Build rapport by looking at things from the customer's perspective.
- Look at how your customer behaves—adjust your behavior accordingly to accommodate their behavioral style.
- Three Types of Behavioral Styles
    - ✔ Visuals = 60% of the population is this type. Relate to the world through pictures and visuals.
    - ✔ Auditors = Relate to the world through sounds
    - ✔ Kinesthetic = Relate to the world through touch and feelings

- No matter how skilled a salesperson you are and how hard you try, some prospects just aren't buying. Know when to say NEXT.
- Follow-up Thank You, recognition and congratulation notes

INVESTIGATIVE PRINCIPLE #7
Develop the Qualifying Instinct

CLUE:

The Secret of a Great Investigator is to Become A Focused Fact-Finder!

"Without proper qualification, you're like a ship without a sail--going nowhere."
Omar Periu

What Is Qualifying?

Think of qualifying as a step-by-step process of discovery. This is the time to discover information about your customer by asking excellent questions and practicing precise listening. If you are a more experienced investigator who is used to qualifying the old-fashioned way, through interrogation, it's time to change your ways. Selling has become a sophisticated business with salespeople who are sensitive to the customers' needs and customers who are savvy to the salesperson's techniques.

Why Qualify?

Although it takes more time in the beginning, qualifying your customers actually saves you many frustrating hours in the long run, working with a customer who cannot be sold. No matter what some books or trainers tell you, nobody can sell to everyone. What they can do is discover the prospect's needs and wants and find the best possible match, demonstrating skills and abilities as the problem-solver and expert advisor. Salespeople should also understand that you can't sell just anything you happen to like to anybody with whom you come into contact. If that were the case, the profession of selling would have an even worse image in the minds of the general public. Let's face it, there are going to be some people who just can't be sold. When you qualify the prospect, you learn that up front, or at least very early in the selling process.

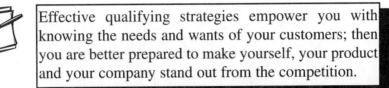

Effective qualifying strategies empower you with knowing the needs and wants of your customers; then you are better prepared to make yourself, your product and your company stand out from the competition.

Your customers will be impressed with your knowledge, but there is more to qualifying than that. Don't forget the personal side of the sale. Pay attention to the customer's personality type; prepare a value statement about your product or company that will earn you the right to meet with that customer. It could be something like this: "Mr. Jackson, there is a reason why your top three competitors allow my company and I to serve their needs. It's because our product has been proven to increase their overall productivity in the areas of . . ." Try to hit on the areas of concern you have recognized in his personality type. If there is an ego involved, include what your product or service will do and how good it will make him look to his superiors. If the person is very detailed-oriented, include some statistics or percentages that you can back up with proof letters or survey results. Get the picture?

Qualifying the customer will also eliminate many objections that arise from improper investigation. For example, concerns with budget, decision-makers, size, color, amount, delivery, service expectations, competition, etcetera should all be learned during the qualifying process.

All those objections can then be addressed or avoided altogether during your presentation if you take time to properly qualify your prospects.

Create A Motivating Environment for A Successful Sale

As an investigative salesperson, you'll discover during the qualification stage what will motivate your customer to own your offering. Few people are motivated to own the same product for the same reasons. It's your job to uncover the prospect's reasons for being interested in or needing your product or services or identifying their "hot buttons" and the special benefits you and your product can bring to them.

Remember, don't tell—ask.   Since owning any offering is an emotional process, sell with passion and emotion. Believe passionately in your product and in yourself. Be enthusiastic about the possibilities of developing a long-term relationship with this particular client. Let that enthusiasm show in your attitude and actions.

> You'll never know what will motivate your customers without first asking qualifying questions and listening carefully to what they say they need and want.

Ask them questions that generate excitement about their company and its current project for which they need your product or services. Encourage them to share their feelings and emotions by showing your sincere interest. You may say something like, "Mrs. Black, I'm so fascinated by your business. Tell me, how do you handle . . .?" As she answers, make notes, then comment on her answers to demonstrate your interest. What's next? Ask another question about her response, of course. Once you have her on a roll, you'll just need to give encouragement and feed back to be certain you're gathering the necessary information.

Okay, Now That You Know Why You Should Qualify—How Do You Begin?

You really begin qualifying customers before you ever meet them. In the research stage of planning, you'll want to anticipate their needs and concerns. Close your eyes and actually visualize how excited they will be when owning your offering. Look into the future and see them saving time and money and being much more productive because they made the decision to own your product and service. During the call, begin asking qualifying questions after the rapport-building stage of the meeting—before you begin your presentation.

Once you're with the client, begin by asking permission to ask them some questions. Ex: "In order to know exactly what you need, Mr. Prospect, I'd like your permission to ask you a few questions that will help me better understand your situation. That's alright with you, isn't it?" Always assume this will be okay. By asking for permission, you have established them as the expert in their field and you as a respectful salesperson.

Who Can Help You Qualify?

Listed below are people or sources that can assist you in the qualifying process. Some of them you may have used before, so continue to do so. Some may seem so simple—like going to the library—that you feel they are almost too elementary to discuss. However, did you know that less than three percent of the population actually possess a library card? Be counted in that three percent. Getting a card is free, and there are literally millions of dollars and volumes of resources available to the cardholder. Why would a professional person overlook or bypass such a great tool? Rather than take for granted that you are currently practicing all of these qualifying methods, I thought a list of some sources would be helpful.

- Your company
  - ✔ Learn about other clients in similar industries or of similar size and discover how your company helped them.
- Associate salespeople and peers
  - ✔ Ask how they would handle your current situation.
- Your prospect's own customers and clients
  - ✔ If you know that your prospect's company buys materials from your supplier, meet with your vendor and ask questions about that prospect. They may have some valuable inside information.
- Local library
  - ✔ When in doubt, go directly to the information desk with your questions. They will direct you to the best resources.
- Managers
  - ✔ Ask your manager for information on the prospective client or a connection who may be able to assist you.
- Trade magazines
  - ✔ If you're approaching a particular industry, locate their industry publications and read about the latest news or challenges they face.
- Newspapers
  - ✔ When prospecting in the local area, know current, local events for rapport-building to understand specific client challenges such as zoning changes, construction that may affect traffic flows, etcetera.
- Competitors—yours and your prospects
  - ✔ The object is to learn things about the prospect's competition that were previously unknown. Then you increase your status with that company

from salesperson to consultant or advisor. Of course, knowing your own competition is required as well.

- The Internet
  ✔ Don't be intimidated by this powerful tool. Instead, harness its power and use it to create new sales opportunities. It's as easy as using a "card catalog" in the library. Rather than wandering row upon row of bookshelves, all you do is push a button on your keyboard and the information is yours.

There can be many other sources to assist you in the process of qualifying, but the most important step is beginning the process in the first place. Since listening is such an important tool in qualifying, you may want to review Chapter Four to strengthen your listening and observation skills.

Listening is much different from the interrogation tactics employed by yesterday's salespeople. If you interrogate instead of qualify, you will simply render yourself ineffective in today's marketplace and open the doors for your competition. No matter how effective you may think these tactics have been in the past, you're kidding yourself if you think today's executive will sit meekly by, giving you endless time while listening to poorly prepared, irrelevant questions.

> As you review all the resources available to you, make notes and develop questions you will want to ask the prospect. If you make a habit of developing questions as you go, you will often discover the answers on your own through the next phase of research.

The more you know, the better your chances for success.

Qualifying for the Highest Value

There are proper discovery strategies used to qualify, and definite methods you should avoid. There are also degrees of qualification that salespeople in the "selling zone" achieve. The top level is called qualifying for the "highest-value." By this I mean, if you have a customer who needs one type of product or service you offer, but you realize their true needs are those which your deluxe product or upgraded service package provides, you owe it to your customer and yourself to meet their needs. Don't just take the easy way out and make the quick sale. By going for the highest-value offering, your customers will experience greater long-term benefits and a decreased investment potential for the future. They'll also appreciate your desire to put their needs before your own. It may have been a quicker and easier sale to take the sure thing and run with it, but, instead, you researched their needs and were willing to present the best product and service to address those needs. You practiced investigative selling.

That's the difference between the average and the exceptional salesperson. The superstar salesperson will continue to discover needs and wants in case there is another line of products or services that offer greater benefits to their customers. Think about it, you may have already sold to them before and given them excellent service, so why wouldn't they take a few moments to listen to an offering that could give them even greater value? If you haven't done business with them before and you still try to upgrade them, they'll know you're looking out for their best interests. If you don't give them the highest value for their investment, they'll soon feel you mislead them, and move to your competitor.

This is where the superstar salesperson begins to differentiate himself or herself from good old average Joe. Not only are the superstars looking to uncover wants and needs, but they also look for ones that bring the most benefit to both their customers and themselves.

Don't forget, once you have made the sale, this is the easiest time to go for other higher-value opportunities, like add-ons and upgrades.

Begin the Qualifying or Discovery Process with Yourself

Before you can successfully discover the wants and needs of your prospects, you should be examining your own objectives, your willingness to pay the price of success and your ability to properly prepare. First you have to be able to truthfully make these two statements:

1. I **will** do what it takes to get into the "selling zone."
2. I **know** I can do what it takes to get into the "selling zone."

Statement number two is easy to achieve with a lot of work and dedication. The first statement, however, is critical to your continued success as a salesperson. Are you **willing** to do what it takes to be a successful salesperson? Let me tell you, your willingness is a big consideration, just in the qualifying or discovery step of the sales process alone. The following are a list of ten statements you should make if you are determined to succeed in sales.

I **will** continually do the following:

1. invest the time required to learn about my own company and its products and services.
2. ask questions of my peers to discover their proven techniques and strategies.
3. make a monetary investment in continued education and training in order to become the best. Tom Peters says, "Three percent of your yearly gross income should be invested in education."
4. research my competitors and discover how they and their products and services differ from me and my company's offerings.
5. practice learned strategies and internalize the selling phraseology and proven techniques until they become second nature to me.
6. look rejection in the face and move on to the next opportunity.
7. accept the fact that even when I've done all that is required to put me in the "selling zone," I am not going to win every prospect and close every sale.
8. admit to my prospects that I don't have all the answers, but I will certainly find the answers and deliver them back within a short time frame.
9. make only those promises that I know can be kept, and win the prospect's trust and confidence through my demonstrated knowledge and insightful questions.
10. consistently do all these things on a call-by-call basis to maximize my success results and minimize my customers' confusion and frustration during the decision-making process.

Going Through the Six "KNOWS" To Get the "YES"

To be successful at the qualifying or discovery stage, you have to be a salesperson in the KNOW.

There are six KNOWS that will help you get a YES. The six "knows" are <u>know</u> yourself, <u>know</u> your product, <u>know</u> your competitors, <u>know</u> your customers, <u>know</u> your plan, and <u>know</u> you can succeed.

Let's break it down one step at a time so you'll be the most highly qualified salesperson calling on that prospect.

1. _Know_ *Yourself*

Knowing yourself means both personally and professionally. First of all, you should know exactly what you want and expect from the selling profession. What are your long- and short-term goals and objectives? One of the most important things to consider when experiencing self-discovery is your most dominant character trait. What type of behavior do you display that your customer may find annoying or prohibitive? Then, when you have discovered your personality type, ask yourself if you are willing to take control (or establish self-mastery) over your own behavior in order to serve your customers better.

We have talked about different personality styles in Chapter Six, and I'm counting on the fact that you have now qualified yourself and discovered just what type best suits you. In other words, what is your dominant personality type? Take a look at the labeled illustration and its explanation below to help you identify your own personality or behavioral type:

Personality Behavioral Types Quadrant

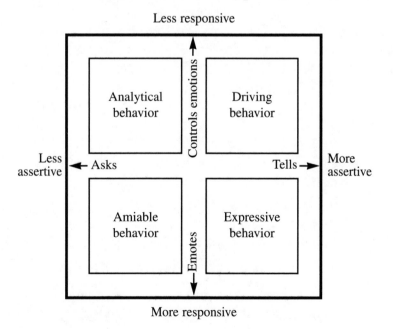

1. Analytical: task oriented; perfectionist; loves facts and figures

2. Driver: direct; dominant and controlling; fast talker and thinker; self
                 contained
3. Amiable: focused on relationships; supportive and loyal; attentive and
                 sensitive
4. Expressive: interactive conversationalist; friendly and talkative;
                 spontaneous and intuitive

> Now that you have identified your dominant type, you need to consider how to become flexible enough to adapt your behavior to that of your customers.

For example, if your customer is ruled by what he or she can see and feel, you will find it valuable to present all your company's tangible facts and figures for them to see on visual aids materials, video and/or feel by demonstration. By this time you may have noticed that some prospects love to have you do that and some sit impatiently watching their wall clocks and asking seemingly intrusive or irrelevant questions about you and your offering.

What these customer behaviors may indicate is that they learn differently, or they may have a much different personality type than your own. If you are rather analytical, with a need to go through what can be a tedious procedure of presenting company facts and detailed product features, don't make the mistake of believing your potential customer feels the same way. Maybe the prospect is a personality type that simply needs to hear about you and your product and make a decision from there. All the tedious facts and figures may be considered time-wasters to this prospect. What should you do? Skip all that tedious stuff; they don't want to hear it. They want to get to know you better. They want you to discuss the benefits of using your products and services.

> It's your job to adapt. Without adapting your personality to theirs, how long do you think they will patiently wait for you to satisfy your need to profusely explain, before addressing their need to learn what your product and service will do for them? Not long, I can assure you!

Let me tell you a little story that may help you to understand what I mean about the importance of listening and observing, about adjusting your behavior to someone else. Ever since I was a child, I have had a very driven nature. I wanted what I wanted, and right now would sometimes be too late to satisfy me. On the other hand, my father's personality was much more direct. What I could count on from dad, like many salespeople do with their customers, is fairness. He always wanted what would benefit not only him, but his loved ones as well, and he was willing to wait for the right opportunity to come along. As much as I loved my dad, like any other normal nine-year-old son, it was my job to point out to dad when he needed to accommodate my needs, right?

As a small child, dealing with a language barrier and living in a strange country, at first I had few friends besides my older brother, Ed, and my parents. Most of the time what I provided for the other neighborhood kids was curious entertainment. Some of the residents of my town were unaccustomed to anyone new moving into their close-knit community. A whole family of Cubans who looked, acted and spoke so differently was uncomfortable for some of the townspeople and their children. All but the very open-minded refused to be neighborly to my parents and forbade their children to play with my brother and me.

Ed was a great older brother, but he was often busy working in the garage with my father and, of course, that left me with no playmate. I felt as though nobody understood my loneliness. My parents had other, more immediate worries of providing for the family. My brother had his responsibilities with dad. I had nobody except the small boy in the mirror, and I was getting awfully bored with his company.

One day, a neighborhood boy, Larry Ley, brought me to his home. He had a little matt-haired, flea-bitten puppy that looked about as friendless as I did. For some reason, I felt I just had to have that puppy and Larry had half a dozen more just like him, anyway. I wrapped him in my coat to protect him from the gently falling snow, and carried him home to present him to my father.

I would have some pretty tall explaining to do in order to convince dad that this little dog would be the watchdog for my father's garage. I planned to first describe its mighty bark and ferocious growl. I would tell dad about its ability to defend and protect our family business from prowlers and looters. There would be no need for dad to wake in the middle of the night and walk out in the cold at the far corner of our property to check the garage. After all, we had Rin Tin Tin to do it now. Rin Tin Tin wasn't just any watchdog, he was Joliet, Illinois' version of Hollywood's "All American" watchdog!

You must understand, this convincing job was no easy task when the puppy in question had little to recommend it but the hopes of a nine-year-old boy. First of all, no dog looked less like Rin Tin Tin, the German Shepherd from Saturday morning matinees, than this scraggly cocker mix. You couldn't really tell what color or type this dog was from the filth and fleas that coated its fur. Second, I had never heard more than a soft sigh and a high-pitched bark to empower it with that ferocious temperament it would need to convince dad it could protect and defend. Finally, I couldn't even face, much less tell my dad, the real reason I wanted the dog—I needed a friend.

As I entered the garage my father held his familiar position, deeply bent over the engine of a shiny automobile he had just repaired. He poised his head between where the loud knock and skipping misfire had been just a few days before, listening for anything else that might lay between the lines of fire. My father was good at that, listening to the hidden message between the lines.

I bravely walked over and greeted my father in an eager voice. Hearing an unusual bit of excitement in my tone, my father lifted his head just high enough to see that I wasn't alone in my greeting. The small, ragged puppy inside my coat had begun to instinctively sense that this was an important moment for him as well, and he wanted to do his part in the convincing process.

My response was that of many other salespeople, defeated in their job of selling before they had even begun to implement their strategy. My heart sank and I resigned myself to the fact that I didn't stand a chance of keeping the pup. I was so nervous and wanted the puppy so bad, all I could think to do was start talking. I rattled off about a billion reasons why we needed this puppy, until I had to stop for a breath. I hadn't adjusted my behavior to match my father's calm questioning. As many do in selling, I let my fears rule my tongue.

Dad put his large, mechanic's hand on my shoulder to calm me. "Son," he said, "No way! Who's going to take care of the pup?" "What will this puppy really do for us?" He was expressing his concerns and asking what the benefits would be. Like many of our customers, dad began to answer his own concerns before I had the chance.

"It's obvious that guarding the garage is out of the question unless I want to post my "Beware, Killer Dog" sign outside the garage and have everyone who pulled up double over in laughter!" said dad. "Maybe that's what we need around here anyway." It was an easy statement made at the tail end of an almost sarcastic question. Many customers will do this, link very important statements on the end of ones that seem almost unimportant and even somewhat caustic.

> That's when it came to me. When I stopped talking, stopped telling and simply listened, I knew just what to say.

"It would bring you laughter, dad!" I knew all the telling I had been doing wasn't near as effective as that one moment of listening in order to discover just what dad needed. By stepping back and adjusting my behavior to a calmer, more reasonable self, dad had listened to my words in return. He worked so hard and worried so much about providing for his family; what he really needed most was laughter. Once I got my eyes off my own needs and looked at what it was my dad needed, I succeeded in selling my dad on the puppy idea. From that moment on, Rin Tin Tin was a member of the family and I had a best friend.

Not only had I listened and discovered what dad really needed, but I also created a comfortable environment when I stopped to take a breath and listen to my father's calm words. I mirrored his behavior. I also delivered what I promised—years and years of enjoyment. I really consider this my first great sale. It was a "teachable" moment, and if there is one thing I have always been, it is teachable.

During those few moments as a nine-year-old boy, I had entered the fantastic world of successful selling. What I had done was listen to what my dad wanted, and focus on his wants. Who would have guessed that selling would be so easy? Once you master the investigative strategies in this book, you'll begin to find selling is easier for you, too.

2. _Know_ Your Product

This should go without saying, but some companies have many products, and it is difficult for the beginner salesperson to be an expert on all of them. I suggest you know at least several products that are upgrades and a few downgrades from the product you wish to present, just in case you need to offer your customer an alternative. You should also know what differentiates your product from that of your competition. If your product has features that are inferior to your competitor's product, briefly state them up front and move on to its greater benefits. Really great salespeople can bring up an inferior feature in their product, turn it into a benefit, and actually sell the client on the obstacle.

3. _Know_ Your Competitors

As much as you may have qualified yourself and your prospective customer, if you don't know your competition, you really don't know what you are up against in the selling process.

> How can you claim that your product and service is best for the customer if you are not familiar with the products and services of others in your industry? You can't!

Just as important as knowing your competitors' products is to learn their selling style. While you are at it, discover what services they include in their agreements, how their warranties work, what their service response time is and whose handling your same territory for their company? Knowing the styles and habits of the "other" salesperson can be as valuable as knowing about his or her product. If your competitor is in your territory only once every six weeks and you are there every four weeks, be sure the client hears about your higher level of personal service.

It is perfectly acceptable to ask your customers if there are any other companies they plan on contacting about their needs as they relate to your offering. Most of the time, they'll be happy to tell you the names of several competitors they plan on contacting, or they may give you a clear indication right then that you are the only one with whom they will be talking. If you know customers will be calling on your competitors, now is the time to differentiate yourself, your company and your product and services.

Don't worry if you are the first in the sales sequence. That simply means you'll have every opportunity to set the standard by which everyone else will be compared.

> Make it your job to know what your company can offer that others cannot. Then create a need in the customer to own that particular offering, today. Turn your strengths into immediate needs of your clients.

4. *Know Your Customers*

Of course, when you approach selling from the customers' perspective, knowing your customer becomes one of the most important aspects of the sale. Here are some questions to ask the customer that will give you some insight. Become the investigative fact-finder.

Don't Forget

Remember, **buyers will tell you how they want to be sold—all you have to do is learn to listen!**

- What does the customer own or not own now?
- What are the benefits, features, or services they do or do not have now?
- Given the chance, what features, benefits and services would they have if they made the decision to own today?
- What specific issues must be fulfilled in order to make a final decision?
- When do they need what you are offering?
- What is their budget for your offering?
- What type of investment or financing will they need?
- Who else is involved in the decision-making process?

While you are asking all these questions, be aware of the customers' behavior and body language. What is their dominant personality trait? Make sure that your responses to their concerns accommodate that trait. For instance, if they are expressive, be sure to fully explain your product and give them plenty of opportunity to express their concerns. If they are drivers, make sure that you keep the conversation moving at a pace where they feel comfortable, and take notes because their no-nonsense approach will probably require quick responses and a lot of information within a short period of time. If the driving personality begins to look impatient, let them know right up front how long your presentation will be.

5. *Know Your Plan – But Still Be Flexible*

You really should have two plans so you can move to Plan B in case Plan A doesn't work. It's always better to prepare for the worst and expect the best; that way you are never caught off guard. There are two things to focus on in your planning:

1. What is your objective for the contact?
2. How do you plan to meet that objective?

It is important that your customers know these two things also. They need to be clear about why you are there and what benefits you can bring to them. Don't assume they know if you haven't clearly stated those two things. The best way to make sure someone gets your message is to deliver it, in person, face-to-face. After the message has been delivered, question their understanding of it.

6. *Know* You Can Succeed if You've Done the Other Step Properly (Know Your Outcome)

If you do not know in your heart of hearts that you are capable of success, what are you doing making this contact in the first place? Do you really have the time and energy for dress rehearsals? I don't! I can honestly say, I have never been on a call where I didn't truly believe I could possibly make the sale and know that my customer would benefit from owning my product or service as much as I would from selling it. Know your outcome according to the sales cycle of your specific product and service. Then make the decision that your prospective customer will own. Does it work every time? NO! You will sell more with this kind of positive thinking, however.

 If your self-confidence is shaky, do something to lift your self-esteem. Read books, watch videos and listen to tapes or C.D.'s. When I'm feeling a bit unmotivated or defeated, my spirits can be picked up by popping a cassette or video tape in and listening to it as I work out in the morning. The more they encourage me to do what it takes to be successful, the faster I get on my bike or the more weight I bench press. Before you know it, I'm pumped for the entire day.

If it has been an exceptionally difficult few days or week, I go to my inventory of achieved goals that I keep in a goals notebook. It has been a great tool to help me recapture those strong, positive emotions of a big sale I may have made a short while back. Once you begin to see all your accomplishments stacking up in that notebook, who wouldn't feel confident and eager to repeat the performance? Sometimes I will be looking through it and come across a goal I thought was exceptionally difficult to achieve at that time—now it seems so reachable. When this happens I look forward to adding the upcoming sale to my list of achieved goals and looking back on it after a few months with the same feelings of amazement.

There is no better way to increase achievements than to keep a record of past achievements. Once you believe in your own success, you're half way there. You'll already be on your way just by believing yourself capable of being the best salesperson you know.

In the next chapter, I'm going to introduce you to the steps in preparing powerful presentations. Believe me, if you haven't properly qualified your prospect, it won't matter how powerful your presentation. You'll be wasting your breath! In fact, without qualification, there is really no way your presentation will be powerful to that particular customer because you won't have known what his or her specific needs were without going through the qualification process. That's the thing about selling. It's a step-by-step process that needs to be practiced and implemented in sequential order. At this point let me encourage you to review any areas in which you still feel weak. Review one step at a time and then go out in the field and practice what you have learned.

Make it your own. Don't feel as though you must read this entire book before implementing its principles. In fact, that is probably not the way to read and digest all of its magic moments. If you strengthen part of your investigative selling techniques and continue to read about the remainder, you'll still be better off than before.

Another suggestion, if you try to skip the fundamentals, a word of warning: Investigative selling is based on learning and practicing the fundamentals.

In order to receive full benefit from my years of studying, observing, listening and learning, I had to keep returning to the basics, the fundamentals of selling. Let me share a secret with you—SO WILL YOU!

SUMMARY POINTS

- First qualify, qualify, qualify and know you are willing and able to be a professional investigative salesperson.
- Go through the five "knows" to get a "yes"

  1. Know yourself

  2. Know your competitors

  3. Know your customer

  4. Know your plan

  5. Know you can succeed—know your outcome

- Who can help you qualify?

  ✔ Your company

  ✔ Associate salespeople

  ✔ Prospects

  ✔ Libraries/Bookstores

  ✔ Company sponsors

  ✔ Managers

  ✔ Trade magazines

  ✔ Newspapers

  ✔ The Internet

INVESTIGATIVE PRINCIPLE #8
Investigative Salespeople Make Powerful Presenters

CLUE:

Continually Close from the Moment You Open Your Mouth All the Way Through The Presentation. Remember Your ABC's--Always Be Closing!

"If you don't control the presentation from the beginning, you'll never get control of it when it's time to close."
Omar Periu

To most salespeople, the presentation is where they feel most comfortable, where they have the opportunity to outshine their competition, where they can finally impress customers with their knowledge, solutions and well-stated benefits. If the presentation is what most salespeople consider their strength, why do so many sales opportunities fall apart at that very point? It's simple, really! Although salespeople may perceive themselves to be terrific presenters, their perceptions are often flawed. To make sure you don't number among the ranks of the mislead and discouraged, I'm going to talk to you about presentations—perhaps like no other individual has talked to you before.

It has been my experience that presentations usually suffer from the extremes. If a new salesperson is presenting, he or she may have the extreme enthusiasm and excitement that is necessary to deliver a great presentation. What they lack is knowing and implementing the fundamentals, like planning for the presentation, confirming the appointment, anticipating concerns, developing phraseology that addresses those concerns and controlling the presentation through a structured process of probing questions and insightful responses.

On the other hand, veteran salespeople may have prepared to the extreme. They may have done all their homework and developed an incredible presentation; however, they lack that fresh, raw passion of the newcomer. Because their presentations are old hat to them, their method of delivery becomes boring to the prospect who is no more excited about hearing the offering than that tired out salesperson is excited about presenting it.

With these two extremes, is there any hope for a happy medium? Are all experienced salespeople destined to become worn out and tired presenters? Not by any means, and that is exactly what this chapter is about. In the next few pages, I'll show you how to structure a great presentation, talk to you about personal delivery, teach you about PACE (Poise, Articulation, Count Two, and Eye Contact), and uncover the five steps of learning how to give powerful presentations. Since we've got a lot of work ahead of us, what do you say we get started!

So, What Exactly Is A Presentation?

A presentation can be a formal 45-minute interaction between you and many prospective customers, or it can be a 5-minute one-on-one. A presentation is simply your opportunity to position yourself and persuade your customers to see, hear and touch and believe in the superiority of your product and service.

One of the important things to remember is that your presentations will almost always continue as they began. If you begin a presentation with the customer taking charge—saying, "Oh, I'm sorry. You'll need to do this in about ten minutes because I have to be across town within the hour," you've lost control of your presentation. TAKE CHARGE!

> If you cannot effectively do your presentation in ten minutes, obligate them to reschedule the presentation. Don't sell yourself and your product and services short.

I can't emphasize enough how important it is for you to establish control in the very beginning.

By control, I don't mean talking nonstop or browbeating your customers. What I mean by control is staying focused on your objective. What is your objective for this particular presentation? In this case, don't look at the word "control" as a negative. Perhaps this is a situation where we should use the word "manage," instead. How? By staying in the character

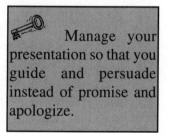

Manage your presentation so that you guide and persuade instead of promise and apologize.

of the investigative salesperson. Ask questions, listen, observe, take notes and gather information. When you can consistently do these things, you won't have to worry about who is in control of the presentation—you will be managing your presentations and your business.

My brother, Ed, is a natural at managing businesses. Even when we were children, Ed could always figure out a way to sell more chocolate bars for high school band than any other kid in school. Of course, he rarely did the actual selling himself; he simply bribed me with some of the chocolate bars. He let me test them and see how great they tasted, got me emotionally involved and then turned me loose on the unsuspecting neighborhood.

I'd go up to the door with a great presentation. Even at that age, I definitely knew how to set the stage. How could the prospective customer resist? First of all, I always looked as neat as a pin. I'd knock on their doors, prepared with a smile and a candy bar in my hand. Customers would open their door to a cute, determined, business-minded little kid with an entire box full of candy to sell so that his school band could earn this or that. When they opened the door I would just hand them the candy bar and say "Here." It was simple, one-step selling.

> I just assumed the answer would always be "yes," and most of the time it was.

Once they had it in their hand, they rarely refused to buy. Instead, they would laugh a little at my simple, straight forward approach and ask for two or three bars.

I could canvas a neighborhood in less than thirty minutes and be back for another box. My brother looked like a hero, and I did all the selling. It wasn't really work for me; I loved meeting all the people and getting the praise from my brother when I came home with another empty box. The chocolate bars weren't half bad, either. Not only did I learn about business management, but I discovered the rewards of selling as well!

Plan to Present

This is a two-fold process. Whenever you plan to present, you must prepare **yourself** as well as your presentation. One is dependent upon the other for maximum success. After all, who's going to recognize the benefits of owning your product or the impact your specialized service will have on increasing productivity levels or turnover time if you have not personally prepared yourself as the presenter? The following are the steps I go through to prepare myself for a power presentation:

Ten Steps of Mental and Physical Preparation for an Effective Presentation

1. I tell myself I'm a great presenter; I'm a Great Presenter; I'm a GREat PRESenter; I'M A GREAT PRESENTER, until my belief and inner power builds and I can feel and believe the words! One important thing to remember about positive affirmations, though.

    > Positive affirmations must be backed by emotional belief!

    If you simply repeat empty words you don't believe, they'll do precious little for your presentation. You'll leave your customers with those same negative feelings about you that you yourself may believe to be true. Get rid of those negative feelings about yourself. When you practice saying positive affirmations, say them with conviction, enthusiasm and energy until you believe what you are saying. It's really a simple process of believing in yourself and behaving in a way that encourages your customers to believe in you, too.

2.
    > I make sure that 80 percent of what I'll be saying is appealing to the customers' emotions (the why) and 20 percent to their logic (the how).

    Why? It's a known fact that people buy based on emotions rather than logic. They own more of what they **want** not what they **require**. **How?** I make owning my product or service fun and exciting by using words that are extraordinary and descriptions that give them a visual image of themselves as happy owners.

3. Delivering the message.

    > There are two important elements of the message. What you say and how you say it.

Being strong in content but weak in delivery won't make you a superstar salesperson. Remember, you don't have to tell me how you feel; make your actions so loud they will be deafening.

That's what salespeople do to their customers when their presentations are poorly delivered or inadequately planned. They cause the customer to be focused on something other than ownership. Who would care how articulate you were if your message was all polish and no proof? Offer your customers testimonials from satisfied customers. Inform the customers of other situations where your product and services brought success (state the specific improvements and benefits) to XYZ Corporation. Be careful when presenting your message.

> Don't be a master at the promise and a moron at making the promise good!

4. Get out of yourself. Be external. Empty everything you've got into your prospective customers and fill them with your words, gestures, feelings and beliefs. When you are external, you'll be able to better evaluate the correctness of your gestures and feelings.

> The more you can put yourself in the shoes of the customer because you are externally examining what is being said and done, the more able you will be to offer them relevant benefits and rewards when they use your product and service.

Being external means   focusing on the customer, the environment and the entire selling situation, not just on your performance!

5. Create a presentation table of success in selling.
    • The legs of support are…
        ✔ Products and services – Have you targeted the customers most suited to your products and services? Are you speaking to the decision-maker, and when will he or she be ready to buy?

✔ Company – Is the company in a position to own your offering? Is your company able to supply the product and service that best suits your customers' needs?

✔ You – What is your knowledge base? What are your qualifications? What training have you received? Are you the best in the company to represent your client? Do you have an unshakable faith in your ability to get the job done? Is your focus what is best for the customer? How is your attitude? Do you believe in your products and services?

✔ Closing the Sale – Did you make recommendations and ask for the business? Can they own today? Have you asked for the order?

6. I say to myself that my presentation is powerful and effective, and my customers need to hear what I have to say. If you have a great offering, your attitude and words have to convey that as well as your product, service, or company. To get them to listen and value what you have to offer, you have to value it yourself; you have to make them feel (remember we're dealing with an emotional situation here) like they have invested their time wisely. The customer should be the one saying "I'm so glad you came by today."

7. I visualize who I want to become. I'm a rare DIAMOND, developed through the survival of incredible sales pressure. There is only one like me. I have learned a lot about diamonds through my wife, Helen, who is the number one salesperson in her fine jewelry store, I might add. She once explained to me the extreme pressure a diamond goes through in order to create that rare and unique beauty. More than anything else, it's the pressure that gives the diamond strength and clarity.

After hearing Helen's story on what diamond's go through, I better understood what creates excellence in sales.

> If you want to be a salesperson with strength and clarity of purpose, if you want to be a DIAMOND, then you will have to be able to withstand the pressure of this business.

8. I imagine what customers will feel like when they own my product and service. This is how you can tap into that emotional buyer. Sell through the senses. Describe your product and how it will fit their wants and needs so thoroughly and with such enthusiasm that they feel as though they'd be missing out if they didn't own it.

9.

> I become an investigator—get into character, ask questions, fact-find and gather information.

It always comes back to this, doesn't it? You can do all the rest very well. You can create excitement, get external, believe in yourself, the whole nine yards. Bottom line—if you don't get feedback or gain insight by asking questions; if you don't take notes and gather information, you won't remember half of what transpired during the entire   process. Instead you'll be caught up in yourself, your own performance, or just the excitement of the sale. Important selling signals and objections or concerns that need to be addressed will pass you by because you failed to be the investigator.

10. I enjoy the challenges of the selling process. This takes no explanation. Just have a good time and stop worrying so much about all those outside pressures.

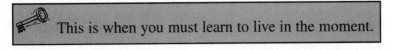

> This is when you must learn to live in the moment.

I saw a movie not long ago where one of the characters became overwhelmed with all the work that needed to be done. Then she was reminded that people were being helped, and she realized the job could be completed by handling **one** issue at a time. No matter how much you like to believe you can handle many different things at one time, you are kidding yourself. The true talent of an investigator is how well he or she can focus, one thing at a time, on the task at hand!

> I've always held to the philosophy: *"If you're not happy where you are—you'll never be happy where you ain't!"*

Enjoy your work, your day, because if you work the kind of long hours most of us do and are unhappy doing so, how will your personal life bring you any satisfaction? Life is short—enjoy what you do!

Keep the P.A.C.E. of the Presentation

If you mumble and stumble your way through a presentation, nobody will ever know—know that you planned, that is. What they will notice, right off the bat, is how tedious and ineffective your efforts were. One of the first things I would like to share with you in preparing yourself for the presentation is a little system I've used for many years called P.A.C.E. Here is what it stands for:

P = Poise

This is the poise you have from the moment you enter the customer's office, throughout the presentation, and right on through until you leave the meeting. I'll share a short story with you. I used to think the meeting ended with handshaking at the end of the sale. When the salesperson either walked away with a commitment, with a promise for down-the-road ownership, or with disappointment, that was the end of the presentation. But, I was very wrong.

One afternoon, a fellow salesperson and friend shared his experience of doing just that, giving a very thorough and insightful presentation. He organized and delivered a great presentation and closed the sale. The customer was duly impressed. In fact, she was so impressed that she continued to talk to my friend as he walked to the parking lot and got into his car.

Suddenly, the conversation came to a standstill. Like any salesperson worthy of the profession, he realized a drastic change in the selling climate as he got into his car and drove away. Thinking he was putting too much emphasis on his emotional state, he didn't think much about it until he returned to the office and there was an urgent message to return a call from the customer with whom he had just established that $500,000 account. Five minutes later he hung up in shock at what had just happened. The sale was off, and for what he considered to be the lamest of excuses. However, the more he thought of the customer's reasons, the more he had to take responsibility for the loss. Here's why!

Once the customer saw what a messy car he drove, she called to express her concerns about trusting him with developing a system that promised to organize her company and track her accounts. It was pretty evident my friend was having great difficulty organizing his own life, so why should the customer think his ability to organize her business would have different results? No, the sale was over! Needless to say, my friend listened to and learned from what happened on the presentation call that day. And, although the end results for that call were very hurtful and almost unbelievable, he chose to look at what happened as a learning experience for every one of his future presentations.

From that day forward, he rarely drove a car that wasn't mirror-image shiny. The bottom line about this call was what my friend said he realized through losing the single most important customer he had approached in years—

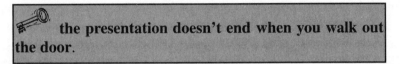 **the presentation doesn't end when you walk out the door.**

Your personal presentation takes place each time you speak face-to-face or phone-to-phone with your clients. Your job is to make sure you are poised and prepared for business at all times, including keeping a clean car, free of all the unnecessary paraphernalia of a busy salesperson.

A = Ability to be Articulate

No! You don't have to be perfect. Remember what I said about waiting to do what needs to be done in order to be successful? Waiting on perfection will keep you inactive forever! Being articulate doesn't always mean you say what's on your mind; but, rather, you keep your mind on what you say. Make sure your language is that of a positive salesperson.

Adopt a straightforward, clear pattern of speech peppered with frequent changes of pitch and tone in order to convey excitement and get your customer emotionally involved with your product and service.

This section also needs to emphasize the importance of giving attention to your pronunciation and volume. It stands to reason that you won't be getting too many main points across to your desired prospects if your lips are so close when you speak that you couldn't pry them open with a pair of pliers. What you have to say is important, so make sure others benefit from hearing your words. Speak and breathe from your diaphragm. Create as big an impression with your speech as you expect to with your presentation.

Articulation is also about the tone of your voice and the rate of your speech. By changing these things, you can put authority into your presentation. Make a first impression as one who is confident and assured that your product and service will best benefit the customer's company. **Remember, it's not what you say most of the time, it's how you say it.**

C = Count Two (One-Thousand One, One-Thousand Two)

Whenever you find yourself getting too excited, simply count two. Make it a meaningful pause. Believe me when I tell you, too much excitement is just as detrimental as not having enough. Customers don't like to be shouted at or slapped on the back when you make a presentation. "Count Two" keeps you calm.

> Whenever you need to regroup, just take a mental countdown.

You may even want to close your eyes for a second if it helps you to focus.

If a customer has just asked you a question you feel unprepared to answer, take a deep breath and count two. It allows you to step back, relax and think. Don't worry that your customer will wonder about your mental state, they'll probably appreciate your thoughtful silence, never recognizing the fact you are just organizing your thoughts. Count two will cover your tracks.

E = Eye Contact

Making eye contact with your customer or customers during a presentation is critical. If you are presenting to a group, make sure you scan the room every so often and make eye contact with everyone in order to keep them involved. I have also noticed that some presenters will often speak to one side of the room. If this sounds like you, an easy way to break yourself of that habit is to turn your shoulders slightly toward the opposite direction and your eyes will follow.

If your presentation requires the use of visuals, you may want to break eye contact with your prospects for a while to look at the visual. Even if you have memorized your visuals, your customers have not. The usual reaction for others with whom you come into contact with during the presentation is to return the eye contact. They will look into your eyes at that time, and that may not be where you want them looking. Direct their vision toward your visuals by looking at them yourself and using a pen to pinpoint topics as you introduce them.

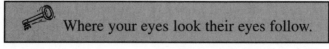

Where your eyes look their eyes follow.

PACE

The entire word stands for your ability to pace yourself during your presentation. When giving a presentation you must always consider the dominant behavioral traits of your customers. I can almost guarantee you that, one day, you will catch a busy executive with a driving trait and feel you must deliver a rather brief presentation. Let's say you define "brief" as 17 minutes. What matters most is how the executive defines "brief." He may have been bored by a presentation that he considers long. It could be that you should and could have shortened your presentation to a single summary fact sheet and a five-minute explanation. The key is to keep on your "investigative hat," watch for clues as to their level of interest and be prepared to make adjustments throughout the course of your presentation.

If you see your prospect getting sleepy, worried over time, doubtful, or even indifferent, and this was not the behavior you saw in the beginning, you need to give them a presentation break. They may be suffering from presentation overload. Ask them if they would like a cup of coffee. Take a short break and build rapport while talking about something that personally interests them. If they are zoning out on you, forget it—after all, you can't teach the unconscious!

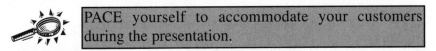 PACE yourself to accommodate your customers during the presentation.

If they want to spend a good deal of time talking about their favorite hobby, be prepared to do so. If they would rather pass on a few moments of introductory conversation and get right into the presentation, you need to be ready to do that, too. Work at the customer's PACE, within their comfort zone. While it helps to build rapport, being the investigative salesperson and discovering your customer's interests or common ground will help you to later close the sale. If your customer is running to deadline on another project and has specifically set aside only thirty minutes for the presentation, impatience may set in during the rapport-building stage. Be flexible!

It's important to be allowed to give your entire presentation, having the client reserve his or her questions for later. However, you'll find clients who want to keep on track with their train of thought and get immediate answers to their questions during the presentation. If that's what it takes to sell them, be prepared enough with your presentation to get yourself back on track after taking a brief side trip to answer their questions.

Become a Power Presenter

Research shows that approximately 80 percent of your prospect's decisions will be based on emotion. However, customers don't walk into a presentation emotionally charged and ready to buy, just to make your job of selling that much easier. In fact, it is usually quite the opposite. Customers know that you are a salesperson.

 In their eyes, your purpose for being there is to make them spend money. It's your job to change the customer's perception about you.

Become the customer's problem-solver instead of simply a money exchanger.

In reality, the purpose of power presenting is to discover. As we've repeatedly stated throughout this book, it's an investigative process. You must uncover existing desires, perhaps create new desires and determine what and how the customers benefit from owning your offering. A power presentation is really the process you use to get you to the close. More than your presentation being the most showy, talked about event of the week, if it doesn't get you to the close, it wasn't effective.

There's no "Best in Show" award given to the year's most glitzy presentation. Your rewards come when you give a power presentation that earns you positive results—a sale.

Structure of a Power Presentation

Those top producers who are consistently in the "selling zone" never tire of repeating an effective power presentation. Sure, they tailor it to customers' wants and needs, but most of the time they tell the same selling story with as much excitement as if they were telling it for the first time. How can they maintain that fresh enthusiasm? They know that at the end of their enthusiastic, new-sounding story everybody will leave the table and live happily ever after. Their customers are happy they have made a decision to say "yes" that will give them the benefits you promised. The salesperson and his or her company are happy to have shared your offering and had another productive day.

Repetition is the name of the game when it comes to presenting.

Not only do you need to repeat a power presentation, practicing and refining it until it's next to perfect, but you also need to repeat important points during the presentation.

Make the dimensions of your presentation 3 x 3. Let me explain what I mean by this. The structure of your presentation should be as simple as information on a 3" x 5" card; therefore, you should have no trouble memorizing it instead of trying to wing it.

I became a professional when I learned my presentation word for word. I remember Tom Murphy evaluating my presentation during the time that I thought winging it was good enough and, once again, Murph gave me this all important advice: **"Who are you kidding?"** If you are winging it like I used to do, I suspect it's as inadequate for you as it was for me. If you've been successful in spite of yourself, just think how much more you'll be able to attain when you practice the following three steps:

1. Tell customers what you are going to tell them.
2. Then tell them in the body of the presentation.
3. Finally, tell them what you told them in the conclusion or summary section of your presentation.

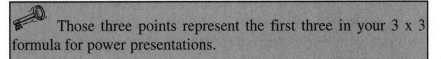

Those three points represent the first three in your 3 x 3 formula for power presentations.

Now, understanding the importance of repetition, plan on repeating your major points at least three times, and that is what the second 3 in your 3 X 3 formula stands for. I say things three times to my customers who, by the way, probably won't have fully understood my point the first two times. Of course, you need to be clever about the way you repeat the information. Vary your wording and your delivery in such a way that they don't realize you are merely restating and reinforcing the same benefit in a different way. I've said it before, but, since there is power in repetition, let me say it again. More times than not, what makes a memorable moment is not what you say but how you say it. So, let's talk about the words to use to create memorable presentation pictures.

Words Will Come and Go, but the Pictures They Create Can Stay Forever
When you leave the presentation:
- Customers should be talking about how articulate and well-prepared you were.
- They should be so emotionally-charged about owning your product or service that they can't wait to see you again because of your power presentation.
- They'll actually look forward to learning what you have to teach them.

If you've investigated their wants and structured your presentation from the customers' perspective, focusing the major points around their wants, you won't have to worry about getting them emotionally involved. One of your concerns, however, should be how to maintain that level of excitement.

Create a lasting image by using descriptive words that stay in the minds of your customers. If your product is speedboats, don't leave your customers sitting at the table looking at a faded or wrinkled picture and a price list of speedboats. Build value in that speedboat! Leave them dreaming about racing the lake at 65 miles an hour with the wind whipping their hair, the vibration of the engines beneath their feet and a crowd of people on shore pointing in their direction in disbelief at their hungry beast of a speed machine. Let them see it eating up the waves from one end of the lake to the other. Have them experience the thrill of turning on a dime with two twenty-foot fins of white water shooting from their dual exhaust. Now that's a picture, wouldn't you say?

Look at the above paragraph and pick out all the action words and phrases that helped to create this picture. In just a few short sentences, these power words were used to paint a vivid picture that will stay with the customer for days after your presentation.

racing at 65 m.p.h.	**whipping**	**vibration**
pointing crowd	**hungry beast**	**speed machine**
eating the waves	**turning on a dime**	**twenty foot fins**
shooting out		

If your customers picture themselves as the stars of speed at their favorite lake, you've probably just made yourself a sale. After you put them behind the seat of that incredible machine, you may even want to show some videos of people racing the lake. If you can discover where they most enjoy boating, it's great to show that particular spot. Even use some still photos that you may have taken of others out on the lake enjoying their boats. Anything that will repeat and reinforce that picture is an effective closing tool.

> So use words that paint long-lasting, emotional pictures in the minds of your customers during your presentations.

The Most Effective and Powerful Presentations
If you want to design the most powerful presentations, you must do the following:
- Know everything about your client.
- Create control by asking questions.
- Build "yes" responses and minor agreements.
- Separate yourself from the competition.
- Use sight, sound, touch, smell and taste.
- Present total solutions and benefits.
- Use positive word pictures.
- Prevent sales resistance by bringing up known objections.
- Respect and care enough about your customers to adapt your behavior in order to accommodate theirs.

Allowing yourself to be weak in even just one area of the presentation is giving your customers a reason to say "no." Work on every weakness until it becomes your strength.

> Get so comfortable with your presentation that the words are easy and the message remains fresh and exciting.

Five Steps To Learning Memorable Presentations that Pack a Punch
If you do the following five things ahead of time and plan for success, chances are great that you'll increase your sales and shorten your sales cycle.

There are five steps to go through to make this happen:
1. listening
2. researching
3. writing
4. saying
5. rehearsing

Let me break these steps down for you a little further so you'll be fully prepared for **power**!

1. *Listening for Clues*

   During the presentation, listen to what your customers or your contacts tell you about their wants and their points of dissatisfaction. Practice active listening, which means taking notes, asking relevant questions and clarifying what you are hearing.

2. *Researching for the Presentation*

   Go to every source you can think of and find research that supports the use of your product or service. Have third-party testimonials ready to present that are from customers who have benefited from using your offering. Include national success stories of company leaders who were unafraid to take that first step to greatly benefit their company. If you are making a personal sale, switch all these things over to the family and the customer's personal needs, wants and issues.

3. *Writing—Take Great Notes*

   Absolutely refuse to depend upon your memory for all the points you want to make in your presentation. In fact, customers are impressed when you come in with strong data to support your points. When you have written down your research, be sure to keep it. If you are calling on other companies in the same field, it will save you a lot of time. Another practice you will find to be a time-saver is to find a research partner within your organization and trade research with him or her. You'll both save a great deal of time and you'll benefit from one another's insight.

4. *Speaking Powerfully and Descriptively*

   Before you incorporate an idea or concept into your power presentation, say the words out loud. Roll them around on your tongue a few times. Make the words comfortable for you to say yet exciting for your customers to hear. This is especially important if you are using unusual words that make customers listen to you because they are not accustomed to hearing such language. **Ex: If you are selling something most people don't picture as being very exciting, like retirement plans, you have to use words that are memorable, such as: "become a retirement giant," "renew your verve and vivacity," or "adopt a live-for-today attitude." "Wouldn't it be great with this program if you could have all your dreams come true in your golden years? You can!"** These types of phrases or words distinguish your customers' retirement years as being those most powerful and active, filling them with positive feelings.

If you don't say these words out loud as you prepare, you may stumble over them when it comes to delivering your power presentation. When this happens, you will create a memorable experience all right, one of embarrassment, which leaves your prospects with a vivid negative picture. Although these embarrassments make for great conversation at the next company social gathering, that's one time you'd probably just as soon not be the hit of the party.

5. *Rehearsing—Practice and Perfect Your Presentation*
    This is the most important part. Remember what I said about the purpose of repetition? Well, repetition serves you just as it will your customers. The more you rehearse your presentation, the easier it will be to remember it when you're under the gun. When those tough objections begin to surface, you'll remember what it was you wanted to say about them. In fact, if you're in the "selling zone," you'll be the one bringing those objections to the surface and getting them out of the way quickly so you can begin to paint your benefits picture.

All the years I studied to be a professional opera singer, I realized the importance of practice. Not just any kind of practice, but the practice of what was right to perfect my voice. For a long time, I thought my voice just wasn't going to allow me to become a professional singer, until my voice teacher pointed out a few truths. Never one to mince words or spare feelings, he said to me one day "Omar, why isn't your voice improving?" He was right! It wasn't improving and I was devastated, but I refused to give up. I told him how much I was practicing the scales, doing everything that I was told to do. So, he asked me to do some scales for him.

It was obvious to him what was wrong with my voice. He told me that I was going too high and too low on the scales. That's why my voice was not improving, even with all the hard work. I wasn't practicing properly! So instead of improving, I was actually hurting myself. As soon as I did exactly what my voice teacher recommended, my voice improved dramatically. He was first to praise my efforts, while still leaving me with the feeling that I could do better.

 I want to do that for you. When you implement the skills you are learning in this book, I want to be the first to congratulate you on your new successes. However, I'll also be the first to warn you about becoming complacent and relying on past successes.

> There is no time during the selling process to bask in past performances.

There is a lot of truth to the statement, **"You are only as good as your last sale!"** If I were to compare building your sales careers to how I built my professional singing career, I'd advise you to practice 'til you think it impossible to deliver one more close, then rest for the evening and wake to look forward to more of the same tomorrow. The day-to-day practice of talents and skills is certainly worthwhile when you get a standing ovation or a closed sale as a result of all your hard work.

How Do Successful Investigative Salespeople Spend Most Of Their Time?

The average salesperson spends 80 to 90 percent of their time in the presentation! This leaves only 10 to 20 percent for all the other aspects of a successful selling career. A powerful presenter spends only 40 percent of his or her time actually practicing the presentation. The remaining 60 percent of the time that salesperson is qualifying and researching to make his or her presentations specific to the customer's needs.

> This means those in the "selling zone" are only spending half as much time on the actual presentation as those who are outside the "zone." What is most impressive, however, is that the "zoners" are managing to turn in over twice the volume in half the time.

That's really a very conservative average. In reality, the productivity of those in the "selling zone" is more like four to ten times greater.

Let me leave you with one last word about the presentation. If you are using visual aids, make **yourself** the most outstanding visual aid in your presentation. Dress professionally, but not to the point that your looks will distract from your presentation. Make your most outstanding accessory the smile you wear on your face. Unfortunately, we are a generation who has forgotten how to genuinely smile. When you can smile, sincerely, your customers will believe you have to be successful to experience that much enjoyment from your work. A smile radiates warmth and caring; it creates an open, willing environment. If you show your willingness to listen, perhaps your customers will be more willing to own. Do you recall my story about Zig Ziglar and that great smile of his? Every time I see him walk into a room, he lights up that room with his smile and presence. Isn't that a wonderful thing—hundreds of thousands of people remembering your words because you treated them to such a friendly smile and warm welcome?

Practice what you have learned in this chapter. Become a powerful presenting machine, ready to generate excitement, emotional involvement and happy new clients wherever you go. Take what you've learned here into every presentation.

Become the expert advisor and make recommendations that will impress your customers with your ability to question, listen and respond with targeted and specific suggestions that will bring positive results to them and their companies.

SUMMARY POINTS

- Continually close from the moment you open your mouth all the way through the presentation.
- Prepare and plan an effective presentation (content as well as delivery).
- Practice P.A.C.E. when presenting and you'll give value to your message and attention to your delivery.
  - ✔ P = Poise
  - ✔ A = Articulation/Speech
  - ✔ C = Count Two/Give Yourself a Breather
  - ✔ E = Eye Contact
  - ✔ P.A.C.E. = Rate and Speed of Delivery

- Become A Power Presenter.
  - ✔ Tell The Customer What You Are Going To Present
  - ✔ Present
  - ✔ Then Review & Summarize Your Presentation

- Create Exciting Pictures By Using Powerful Words
- Use the Five Steps To Learning Power Presentations
  1. Practice Effective Listening Skills
  2. Do Proper Research
  3. Take Notes
  4. Use Powerful Words
  5. Practice and Rehearse

- Last, but Not Least—Learn to Always Confirm the Appointment

INVESTIGATIVE PRINCIPLE #9
Objections Are the Customers' Last Line of Defense

CLUE:

If there are objections, they're interested.

"A no is a maybe and a maybe is a yes!."

Ken Summers

What Is an Objection?

The challenge for many salespeople is that they can't identify a real objection. Objections are enemy #1 to a salesperson because what they do is slow down the decision process. Veterans know them as a "stall" to the sale.

> Objections are statements from customers who want or need to know more information about you, your company or your product and service.

Sometimes they are brought up because of insufficient information. Here's something to remember— objections in the beginning should be stopped or postponed so they won't interrupt your presentation. If the customer says "No, I'd like **Don't Forget** to cover it now." Then you follow the linking process I've created for you to handle their areas of concern. You'll see the linking technique a little later on in this chapter. Just say, "That's a great concern. I plan to cover that in my presentation." Only say that if you know it will be covered. If you don't have that particular information in your plan, a little stall now will give you time to adjust your presentation to see that it is covered.

The customer may not totally agree with you right up front. And, when people don't see things completely from your perspective, they may act disinterested, cautious, inflexible, uncommitted, tense or even argumentative. When they behave this way, they are asking for reassurance, for you to give them more and better information that will allow them to make the right decision. They need you to be patient with them until they understand. The objection phase is no time to be in a hurry. It's a time to continue or further the investigation process—to do more fact finding to determine how to make those objections disappear!

There are only two types of objections:

1. Those that will slow down or stop the sale
2. Those that, if taken advantage of, will move the sale forward

Those that will stop the sale are stipulations to the sale. We'll talk more about those a little later in the chapter. If an objection cannot be overcome, it becomes a stipulation to the close. Some real objections, or stipulations, are ...

- No money or credit
- Not the decision maker
- Ineligibility (such as with some health insurance products)
- NOTE: There aren't many real objections, or rather stipulations, to closing a sale. Although some may be perceived by you and your customers as real objections, with a little work and creativity you'll be amazed at what can be overcome.

Why Object To Objections

Ninety-eight percent of objections are not real and not "nos." If this is the case, what are they? They are maybes, and a "maybe" is usually just a slower route to a "yes."

Knowing this, doesn't it make sense to stop objecting to objections? If you can accept this as truth, you shouldn't worry when you get objections; you should worry when you don't. After all, customers with no objections have no interest in your product and service and no intention of owning it, either.

If customers care enough to object, to challenge the information you have presented, to ask for more proof, to ask you to slow down by giving you objections that stall the sale, they are willing to spend more time with you. Who would do that if they weren't interested in owning? Instead of getting discouraged at the first sign of an objection, you should be settling in and getting comfortable. By objecting, your customers are giving you permission to stay for a while.

Objections are Opportunities—Learn to Welcome Them

By this time, I'm sure you're saying, "Omar, I can accept the fact that I must learn to address objections, but who are you kidding? Now you want me to see objections as opportunities?" Absolutely!

> When customers object, they are about to tell you how to sell them, so get ready to listen carefully!

Omar's Five Steps to Finding the Real Objection

Most salespeople hit an objection and just keep doing the old salesperson routine over and over again, trying to tackle it, stomp on it or overrule it. It is my goal to teach you to stop sounding like a typical salesperson and start being thought of as the recognized expert advisor in your field. You can only be perceived as the expert if you can identify and overcome real objections in a professional manner.

Let me draw you a map of how to find the real objections. If you follow this map, you'll be able to identify the real objections, change the "maybes" into "yeses", or realize the objections that cannot be overcome and move on.

The steps to finding the real objections and overcoming objections are one and the same. Below is your objections map—follow it and you'll find success is your final destination.

Step 1: Your customer is telling you their concerns—listen to them. Timing is important. You may want to postpone the concern by saying **"I'll get to that in one moment."** Or **"That's a great concern. I'll cover that in my presentation."**

Step 2:  Examine the importance of the concern by rephrasing in a question form what was said. Remember, you are an investigator!

Step 3: Find the key to answering the concern. The key is usually found within the concern itself.

Step 4: Verify to see that you have answered the concerns.

Step 5: Go for the close. If a close doesn't work, go back to benefits and features and begin to build "yes" momentum again.

To clarify these steps, let's go into a little more explanation! By the way, this is exactly what you may have to do when your customers don't understand and begin to object to owning your offer. What do you do when this happens? In most cases, clarify your meaning with further explanation.

Step One:  *Listen to Your Customer's Concerns*

If you have done a good job of learning your questioning techniques, you have to do an equally good job listening to the customers' responses. They are telling you what you need to know to move forward in the selling process, so listen to them. Sometimes the answers may not be through verbal clues, but rather through nonverbal clues. Be aware of what they are saying with their body language.

Ex: If your customer says, "**It sounds really good**…" but you never let them finish their statement, you won't know if their sentence was the beginning of an "I want to own your product" or the beginning of an objection. Instead of interrupting and jumping in with "**Great let's figure out when delivery can be made**," hear them out. They may have intended to say "**It sounds really good, but our company needs a bigger machine to handle greater volumes.**" Just think, if you had **heard them out**, you may have been able to take advantage of stepping them up into a bigger machine.

Again, timing is so important. Listen to your customers' concerns, but manage your presentation by letting your customers know you've allotted a certain amount of time at the end of the presentation to cover any unanswered questions. Encourage the prospect to make notes during your presentation about questions that arise so you can address the specifics that might not be a part of the presentation.

Step Two: *Examine the Importance of the Concern*

Once you've heard the objection, and you've heard it several times, you must realize that is has some true merit from the customers' perspective. What you may not know is how important that concern is in your ability to move on with the sale. Once again, you have to investigate. Discover! Reframe the objection in a question form to find out how important the objection. Will this question lead you to discover whether this particular concern is the real one or is it just a method of stalling or slowing down the selling process?

Ex: "Just to clarify my thinking on whether or not this model is appropriate for your needs, would you mind my asking you a question? If it is your belief that model MX5 is insufficient to handle the volume of business you are either now experiencing or will be in the future, it sounds like our industrial model MX10 might be more appropriate for your needs.

Step Three: *Find the Key to Answering the Concern*
Find the key to answering the area of concern by choosing the proper closing technique. If the customer is unwilling to consider your company's larger model, you have to find out why. It could be that all you need to do is show them the facts and figures on the larger machine and let them know how soon they will receive a return on its investment.

Step Four: *Verify that You Have Answered the Concern*
This is such a simple process. You want to make sure that you have put to bed that particular objection. In fact, you must satisfy objections in order to move toward the close, so you ask one little question…
Ex: "May I assume that the information I provided covers your concern?" Or, "Does that answer your question?"

Step Five: 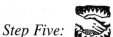   *Close the Sale—Make a Test Close or Move Back into Your Presentation..*

The only thing keeping them from owning your product and service is getting their "yes" answer—when you have answered that objection, go for a test close or a final closing sequence.

Ex: "Mr. Smith, since we have found that the MX10 is just what your company needs to handle its heavy volume, and since we have determined (restate some benefits here), let me get your authorization on the agreement and we'll set up a delivery date for you."

If at this time you run into another objection, you have to start the linking process all over again. You must go back and build toward a strong finish—keep building that "yes" momentum.

Let me give you a possible conversation scenario that will help you to better understand how the skills we've just covered can help you get to the close.

Customer:	"You know what, it sounds good but I'm not so sure that the XYZ machine can meet our production quotas."
Salesperson:	(listen and watch verbal/nonverbal clues) If the customer looks at the math on the paperwork, rephrase in your own words what they've just said. "So let me just clarify what you've said. You're afraid the XYZ machine will slow down your production, is that correct?"
Customer:	"That's right, and if I miss my quotas by just 3 percent, I'm in trouble. That's why I question whether it's worth it to change vendors."
Salesperson:	(ask if that is the only thing keeping them from owning) "Let me ask you, Mr. Buyer, if there was a way I could guarantee you'd meet your production goals every time on time, would you be willing to go ahead with our company?"
Customer:	"Sure!"
Salesperson:	"Okay, you're sure there is nothing else holding you back?"
Customer:	"Well, I'm really not looking forward to all the paperwork I'll have to go through changing vendors. (Now you have discovered perhaps the real objection. The customer isn't

	looking forward to doing all that paperwork and having the hassle in his already busy day.)
Salesperson:	(minimize the objection and hit the "hot buttons" again) "I know what you mean about the paperwork. I'll tell you what, give me the paperwork and I'll fill it out for you. That way, you'll be up and running in just a few weeks. As we've already discussed, you'll reduce the stress on your employees by implementing XYZ's safety features. In addition, the XYZ machine consistently beats your production quotas in all of my clients' plants across the country. Here's a testimonial letter from one of my very successful clients in Cleveland."
Customer:	"For sure, you can guarantee start-up time by the 20th?"
Salesperson:	"Does the 20th fit your schedule the best?"
Customer:	"It sure does!"
Salesperson:	(Nail down the objection.) "Okay, that answers that concern, right? When can you send me the approved paperwork I'll fill out for you?"

The following is a list of opportunities that objections offer to the investigative salesperson. Objections allow you to do the following:
- Spend more time with the customer explaining your product and service
- Point out what makes you and your product and service superior.
- Make the customer comfortable with the knowledge that they will own the best and will be served by the best.
- Offer added value and special services.
- Be a problem-solver, a consultant.

Telling the Difference between A Maybe and a No

The world of sales is such a great challenge. One would think that by doing everything you were supposed to do, the customer would have only two ways to go—either they would own or not own your product and service. If sales were always a black or white issue, that would surely be the case. In sales, however, there is that huge gray area, that no man's land of "maybe." The problem arises when the salesperson can't distinguish a "maybe" from a "no", and with the kind of maybes salespeople can sometimes get, it's no wonder.

For example, did you know the old "**I have to think about it**," is a "maybe?" Or, what about one of my favorites **"I never make a decision without sleeping on it**." Well, unless you're selling mattresses, that isn't what you want to hear, is it? Don't give up; it's still a "maybe." Or even "**I really do love your product,** but **there is just no money in our budget for that right now**." To inexperienced salespeople, these "maybes" sound suspiciously like "nos" and, to hear them signals an immediate "pack up your paperwork there's no reason to be here" response. Average salespeople do just that. They leave the office or let the customer leave their place of business, and they just can't figure out what went wrong.

Here's a story that happened to me that perfectly illustrates what I mean. A while ago, my wife and I decided it was time for a new kitchen. We set up appointments with three different salespeople. The first one came in, measured the kitchen, gave us his vision of what the kitchen would look like, quoted a price, then firmly stated that this was his best price.

The problem was, this man was the first we had spoken to and we felt we needed to get the other two bids on the remodeling job. It wasn't just about price; we wanted to get their ideas on style and color. When we shared our feelings, the man became immediately offensive and said "Okay, I'll tell you what! Because I want to win the company contest and it's the end of the month, I'll drop my price by 25 percent." So, now I'm thinking—how low can he really go? I followed with "I'm sorry, I still have to see the other salespeople. He countered with "If I leave this house, I won't give you the 25 percent off, and I won't be back. The contest is over today. I want to win!"

Well, you can imagine what I told him. He definitely didn't get our business. He may have been very knowledgeable, and his price really might have been the best he could give, but I just didn't want his motive for remodeling our kitchen to be winning a company contest. In fact, I wasn't convinced there was a company contest. I believe this salesperson was relying on gimmicky selling techniques instead of learning strong selling skills to persuade the customers to make a good decision. He certainly wasn't in the "selling zone!" What happened? He gave up and left, and that was another problem this salesperson needed to overcome.

Don't give up on your customers so easily.

> What separates average salespeople from those in the "selling zone" is what happens after the objection.

It's at this time that the real selling process begins. Think about it, **before** you get an objection you're simply sharing a story. **After** the objection is the beginning of persuasion techniques, selling strategies and investigative methods. Don't just make conversation—make sales!

Investigative salespeople know that as serious as these "maybes" may sound, they are really indications that the customer wants something more from them. Successful salespeople have learned to welcome objections. They actually go further than that and invite objections! Why? Because they know without the "maybes" there are no "yeses." "Maybe" is the customer's way of clearing their throat before the "yes."   My friend, Kenneth Summers, CEO of One Valley Bank, says "A no is a maybe and a maybe is a yes." I tend to agree with him, and you should too if you want to see a sharp increase in your sales by persisting through the maybes.

What Causes Objections

Most of the time, objections have little to do with what the customer is actually feeling about your product and service. Objections are more about feelings in general.   Sometimes, like unexplained coincidences that offer opportunities, there is no logical reason for the customer to object. It's not logical—it's emotional. You've done all your homework in preparing. You have demonstrated your knowledge of the product and service through an outstanding presentation. You have developed excellent rapport.

Suddenly, just as you are ready to close, you get an objection. Of course, if you haven't done your homework, there's the cause of your customers' objections. To prevent some of the most common causes of objections, do the following:

- Identify possible objections ahead of time. Then prepare answers to those objections. During the presentation, learn to turn the objection into a benefit. This takes a lot of practice. It all depends on how you word your presentation.

   Ex: If you were a salesperson with a small insurance firm, and size was often perceived by your clients to be a disadvantage, turn size into a benefit. Talk about your ability to provide personalized service, to spend the time with each of your customers until they absolutely understand every component of the policy.

- Develop planned scripts that answer common objections. Notice I say "planned" not "canned" scripts. Know what you want to say when addressing a certain objection so that you sound knowledgeable and calm. Be flexible and ready to make adjustments at all times, but practice basic scripts that will allow you to easily retrieve your response to common objections.
- Practice some closing ideas when those objections may occur. It doesn't have to be a set close, just what you might say should the opportunity present itself. If you know what you would like to say, and overcoming this certain objection will move the sale forward to a possible close, then knowing what you want to do and say ahead of time will be a great tool.
- Come prepared with testimonial letters or on-the-spot references you can provide to the prospective customer in order to give you and your product credibility. Try to choose testimonials or references that would be able to address concerns you anticipate from that particular customer.

> As an inexperienced salesperson, you may be thinking "Not another no!" What did I do wrong?" However, if I've convinced you to think of objections as opportunities, you had better hope they happen!

If you aren't ready to think of an objection as anything but a "no", know this. Studies show that most customers will say "no" at least five times to a salesperson's offering before they finally give a "yes" response and own the product. Can you believe that—five "nos"? Now, think back on all the times you packed it up and left just before your customer was about to say "yes." Couldn't you just kick yourself around the block? All you may have needed was to hang in there for one more "no" or a few more "maybes."

Just When You Thought Everything Was Going Great

Why is it the very time you believe you have done an exceptional job, you get the most objections? It's because you did such a good job and got the customer emotionally involved, getting the customer to care enough about your offering to want to hear more. So give them what they want. Answer the objection. You see, the problem is not in receiving the objections; the real problem is in how you respond to them. Believe me, when you understand what causes them, and you have anticipated common objections and practiced how to handle them, your response will be automatic. Although your answer will be automatic, it cannot sound mechanical. We'll talk about this later on in the chapter for the more experienced salespeople who are still having problems dealing with objections.

A moment ago I said, "If you know what causes the objection..." Well, that is one of the key elements to becoming a problem-solver and an investigator, you must track down the objection's origin. What caused the objection in the first place? I have broken this process down for you by giving you some common causes for concern.

Insecurity and Fear

These feelings don't necessarily have to come from the customer. Objections can occur when the salesperson feels insecure and fearful. Even experienced salespeople have those days when they bumble through presentations as if it were their first time giving it, or they suffer the insecurities and fears of unfamiliarity. That's one misconception that inexperienced salespeople or average salespeople have about those who are successful. The average salesperson believes that top producers who are experiencing great success don't struggle with the same setbacks, fears and insecurities. Wrong! Truth is, they struggle more with fears and insecurities than the average salesperson, and in doing so they learn to overcome them. How? Through preparation!

Improper Qualification

> Many objections that occur are due to improper qualification.

Either the salesperson has failed to first qualify him/herself, or he or she has not qualified the customer.

Let me explain what I mean. If you are in the business of sales and have failed to determine whether or not you are willing to do what it takes to become successful, you may allow yourself to experience incredible pain or personal rejection. You may tend to let that depression creep in when you keep hearing what you think are "nos"! In fact, disillusionment and lowered self-esteem can get their nasty hooks in you when people not near as together as yourself are experiencing very rewarding sales careers.

The problem is, you didn't qualify yourself. Everybody wants to be successful. Everybody wants to have the opportunity to reach the top of his or her chosen field. Why doesn't everybody do it then? They haven't qualified themselves. They are unprepared or unwilling to do what they know it takes to be in the selling zone.

Then there are the situations where the customer has not been properly qualified. Let's face it, it can be difficult enough to close when you have fully qualified the customer. However, if you are not talking to the decision-maker, or if you have failed to practice investigative selling techniques to flush out real inhibitors to the sale, your chances of closing are slim to none.

Almost any salesperson with a lot of enthusiasm and a little knowledge can get an appointment, or entertain a customer who has walked through the doors of a store. It takes a true investigator to gather enough information to qualify that customer.

> Proper qualifying lets the salesperson know when to move forward in the selling process or when to move away from the selling situation all together.

Failure To Build Trust and Rapport Creates Objections

I believe building rapport is most difficult with inexperienced salespeople. Where enthusiasm and energy can benefit them in many areas of the sale, it can often times hurt them during the rapport-building stage. When you are excited and enthusiastic about your offering, all you want to do is jump right in and **tell** them about it. Enthusiasm sometimes makes you forget the importance of **asking**. Suddenly you've completed what you feel was an outstanding presentation, only to come up against challenges that cannot be overcome.

Skipping some of the steps of the selling process is a way to get many areas of concerns and not make the sale. Do not skip any steps to the sales process! Now there is an exception. That exception to skipping steps is when your customer is definitely ready to own and tells you so. For example, if customers say to you after the third step that they want it, don't make them wait until you finish every step to the selling sequence. What do you do? CLOSE THEM IMMEDIATELY!

Failure to Motivate the Customer

If you have gathered all the information like a good investigator, and you have practiced your selling skills until you know them inside and out, you may still fail to motivate the client. As a matter of fact, sometimes this is when you need to focus on motivating the customer the most. It's at these times that your responses can sound too automatic, too mechanical. Customers need to feel as though you are on their side and understand their wants and needs. They want to know you are putting them first.

The failure to motivate is usually a much bigger concern for the veteran salesperson who knows exactly what to say and when to say it, who has done all his or her homework. Why? They've left out the most important ingredient for motivating the client—---**enthusiasm**.

In order to motivate your customer you have to be motivated yourself. Have enthusiasm for your product and your company. Then, as we discussed before,

✔ You must passionately involve your customer. Sharing your enthusiasm means: using uncommon phraseology, unique words that are not often heard from salespeople.
✔ It means allowing yourself the freedom of enthusiastic gestures and facial expressions that sparkle and help you to capture the attention of your customer.

You have to get your customer to want what you are offering, and what you are offering is your energy and enthusiasm as much as your product. You cannot transfer an emotion that you are not experiencing. **Put yourself above an eleven on a scale of one to ten. Coat yourself in layers of positive and take massive and enthusiastic action!**

Common Questions and Areas of Concern

These are probably the easiest objections to overcome. If you have prepared for your presentation, you should be able to answer most of the customer's concerns. If you have visited similar companies, they are likely to have similar concerns. Or, perhaps one of your peers has called on this customer and can help you out when anticipating what some of their concerns will be.

If you do get stumped by an unexpected question which can't be answered in that meeting, be prepared to make a phone call or at least write down the question and assure them that you'll get back to them with the answer. If that means you cannot make the sale today, at least it will go far toward making sure you get another opportunity to make the sale later.

Depending on the product or service you are offering, these common objections may vary, but some could sound something like this: **"Before I make any decisions, I need to consult my partner."** Or **"I really need to think it over for a while."** Even, **"I'm sorry, but we don't have enough money in our budget to cover that kind of expense."** If you have heard these objections repeatedly, you should know to plan for them. In fact, you should be the one to bring up that anticipated objection first and minimize its impact.

Real Objections That Cannot Be Overcome

Like I said before, there are a few objections that simply cannot be overcome, no matter how prepared you are or how much experience you have. These are known as stipulations to the sale. One such stipulation is that the prospect has NO MONEY or NO CREDIT. I have heard of salespeople who were so good at answering objections, they considered every objection a stall or a smokescreen. That may be okay in theory, and it certainly prepares you to handle objections and get past the necessary "nos," but you'll be battle scarred and weary before your time if you believe there is no objection that can actually put a halt to the selling process.

Identifying real objections, or stipulations to the sale, can save you a lot of time and money. After all, if you are spending all your time with customers who cannot possibly own your offering, you're leaving yourself precious little time to spend with customers who are ready and willing to benefit from your product and service.

Keep the value and interest high. Most companies offer add-ons or provide incentives to help their salespeople close the sale. Don't use all of these tools right away. Put some away for a last attempt to close.

This Is No Time To A.R.G.U.E.

No matter how many times you find yourself going through the linking process to answer objections, keep on going if the customer is willing. This is no time to **A.R.G.U.E.** Let me explain what I mean by this.

A   Never **A**chieve your goals at the expense of what is best for your customer.

R   Never **R**esort to domination and control to overcome the objection.

G   Never **G**ive away the farm to persuade your customer to set aside their objections.

U   Never **U**nderestimate the power of investigative selling skills.

E   Never **E**liminate your chances for a return visit by ARGUING the objective.

Omar's Second Method of Handling Objections—It Doesn't Have To Be That Difficult!

I want to give you true value in this book, so I have created a second method for handling areas of concern. The best thing about it is that it isn't that difficult! If you use the same method of linking or handling objections, your customers will know you are using a technique, so here's an alternative method for you.

Step One:

YIELD: You yield by acknowledging the customer and listening to their concerns. **Ex: "You're right Mr. Smith...** Try to bypass! **"I'll cover that in my presentation." Or, "I couldn't agree with you more, and I've covered that in my presentation."**

Step Two:

REPHRASE: After you yield, you turn the objection around with the word "as or and." **Ex: "You're right Mr. Smith, and..." Or, "You're certainly right Mr. Smith, as I said before..."**

Step Three: ⟶

ADVANCE: This is when the sales process moves forward. You advance by introducing new points or revealing more in-depth insight into their specific concerns. **Ex: "You're right Mr. Smith, however, didn't you say product turn-around time is critical to your ability to fulfill your contractual commitments? If so, wouldn't you agree the minimal increase in product justifies the added value we could bring to you by significantly shortening your delivery cycles?"**

Step Four:

CLOSE: This is when you ask for immediate action. **Ex: "Would Monday or Wednesday be better for you?"** Open the door to great relationships. Then, be sure you follow-up so that greater opportunities are yours for the asking.

These four steps should be easy to remember. You can overcome objections through the process of Yield, Turn, Advance and Close!

Ways to Overcome Common Objections
Here are some of the most common objections and ways to overcome them:
- *"I don't just make decisions on the spur of the moment—I like to think things over for a while, weigh the facts!"*
  "That's the smart thing to do Don, but when you've reviewed the facts and discovered that our product/service makes perfect sense to you, am I correct in assuming you'll be ready to make a decision on our product/service?"
- *"I'm really very happy with our current company."*
  "Great! Let me ask you a question. Is this the first company to serve your needs with (product name), or did you make a change from a previous company to your current one?"
  "Oh, I made a change to our current supplier!"
  "And, were you happy with the change?"
  "Absolutely!"
  "Great! Would you agree it is smart to keep an open mind for opportunities that will bring you greater returns for your investment?"

"Of course!"

"That's exactly what I'd like to talk to you about! I give you my word, I won't expect you to make a decision for change that isn't going to dramatically increase your income and bring you a higher yield for your production. If I can do that, you'd be interested in hearing what I have to say, wouldn't you?"

"I guess I would! Yes!"

If you're not the first person to contact this client, you may hear:
- *"I've already talked to one of your salespeople. I'm not interested!"*
  "I really must apologize for the other salesperson's inability to show you how much money you could save while still maintaining your standards of excellence your company is known for. If that was a while back, you may not have heard of our (name new feature) offered with a promotional incentive, have you?"

If you are the first to contact this client:
- *"I've never heard of your company!"*
  "If you don't regularly read the Business or Wall Street Journals, you probably haven't heard of us. You see, Mr. Buyer, we believe our product speaks for itself and have worked hard to create an image that can be supported without high-dollar advertising. Instead, my company chooses to invest its dollars in higher quality products that bring greater benefits to the customers. Doesn't that make better sense?"

  "Yes it does, actually!"
  "Let me provide you with some interesting information on my company (offer them some impressive statistics that are appropriate to your customer)."

You're bound to encounter people who use the excuse of "shopping around."
- *"I like your product, but I'd like to shop around to make sure I'm getting the best price."*
  "That makes sense to me, Mr. Buyer. I'd do the exact same thing in your shoes. Before you make your final decision, could you give me the opportunity to talk to you once more? Is two weeks enough time for you to compare price, or would three fit your schedule better?"

"Two should do it".

"You know, two weeks is just about the time it would take us to prepare your new computer for delivery. If you'll authorize the agreement now, I'll make sure we get your final approval before delivery. That way, by the time you've discovered our company is who you want to go with, you can begin using your new computer immediately." (Assume the sale, hand them the paperwork and say: "Mr. Smith, could I get your approval here?")

Some clients will truly believe they can't afford your offering until you point out how they can.

- *"I would love to have your copier, but I just can't afford it at this time."*
  "I know how you <u>feel</u>, Donna. I <u>felt</u> the same way until I <u>found</u> that by owning our ABC Copier, I could save enough printers charges to cover our monthly investment in the machine. You're not opposed to saving money, right?"

Last, but not least, here's our example from Chapter Six on rapport building.

- *"I just want to know how much it is."*
  "Mr. Garrett, no matter what I tell you right now, it's going to be too much because I haven't been able to show you the value of working with our company and using our fine product." This strategy allows you to slow things down and get back in control."

You'll soon discover after hearing every imaginable objection, that you can answer almost any of them or if you don't have the answer, you can offer to get back with them. In the whole book of objections, there just aren't many that haven't been used before and that can't be overcome!

Remember, most prospects will say "no" five times before a "yes" leaves their lips, so don't leave town just before the "yes" arrives! When you hear a "no," get ready to stay for the long haul until you make the sale.

SUMMARY POINTS

- Learn to like objections—without them there is usually no sale.
- Think of objections as opportunities.
- Use the five steps to finding the real objection.

  1. Listen to your customer.

  2. Examine the importance of their concern.

  3. Find the key to answering the concern.

  4. Verify that you have answered the concern.

  5. Close the sale. If that doesn't work go back to benefits & features.

- Learn to tell the difference between a "maybe" and a "no".
- What are the causes of objections?

  ✔ Insecurity and fear

  ✔ Improper qualification

  ✔ Failure to build trust and rapport

  ✔ Inability to motivate the customer

  ✔ Questions that went unanswered

- Know when to cut your losses and move on.
- Don't argue with your customer. **Never** A.R.G.U.E.

  A = Achieve your goals at the expense of your customer

  R = Resort to domination and control over your customer

  G = Give away the farm to persuade your customer

  U = Underestimate the power of investigative selling skills

  E = Eliminate your chances for a return visit by arguing

INVESTIGATIVE PRINCIPLE #10
Stay Customer Focused and Close the Case

CLUE:

You Cannot Deepen the Relationship
Until You Close the Sale!

"Closing is the easiest thing in the world to do if you have done every other step properly to this point."
Omar Periu

If you've learned and practiced all the investigative selling principles up to this point, and you don't ask for the sale, you've defeated your purpose. You are a professional presenter. Closing is the culmination of everything you've learned. When you pull together everything you've learned, your hard work and determination pay off and you get the final "yes." You should have all of your documentation, facts and figures in line. The "evidence" will support your conclusion, which is for the client to own your product or service.

Definition of a Professional Closer
First of all, let me define for you just what professional closers do. They put themselves in the place of the customer; looking at the selling situation from the customer's perspective and finding the right solution to their wants, needs and issues. If you have done this, a mutually win/win, beneficial close will be the next natural step in the selling process. That is really how I define a professional closer—a super-achiever who persuades and enables customers to have what they want and need by helping them make decisions that they really want to make.

When Does the Investigative Salesperson Close?
The close is a logical step in the sales process. They do it when the time

is right and they are prepared for that timing to be right at any phase of the sale. They take all the steps necessary to lead to the close, beginning with the preparation before they ever meet a client.

Before you even meet your prospect, you should have in mind your key points that will get them emotionally involved in your product and service. During the qualification process, you should be the investigative salesperson, gathering information that will uncover customer wants, needs and issues. This information can be used during the closing to reinforce the perfect fit between your product and service and their needs.

Be the solution to their challenge or need. During the preparation of your presentation, you should be developing a strategy that will address customer concerns in order to offer them answers to their questions. If you've done your job up to this point, closing will be a natural phase of the sales process. Begin the negotiations, and before you know it your customers will be owning your offering.

Selling means gathering information. Then, when the right time comes, you disperse the information back to the prospect, along with your deduction as to how well your product or service will meet their needs.

 So, when do you close, remember the selling ABCs (Always Be Closing)!

If your timing is off, your customers will simply give you an objection in response to your attempted close, and the process continues. Don't be afraid to attempt a close.

Should you be unsuccessful, you haven't blown your entire presentation. You just pick up the selling process again. What should concern you more is if you do an incredible job in all the other areas and never even attempt to close.

Don't worry about when you close.

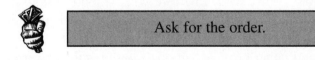
Ask for the order.

Make up your mind that you are going to make a final closing attempt. You are going to find a time to ask for the sale, knowing that you will most likely have to find several occasions to ask for the sale, until you develop your own closing style and proper timing according to your personality and theirs.

Pay Attention to Customers' Buying Signs

It's sometimes difficult to know the exact time to close, so you have to be aware of your customers' buying signs. To do this, you have to practice all the principles I have taught you.

- ✔ You should have developed good rapport and have the beginnings of a trusting relationship.
- ✔ You should be using all the important information that was gathered in the qualifying phase of your investigations.
- ✔ Your presentations and negotiations should have uncovered most or all of the major or real objections, enabling your customers to own your offering.

If all has gone well, you should feel a certain excitement on the part of the customer and yourself—a sort of emotionally charged environment.

Now is when you look for changes that can be considered buying signs.

> ### Buying Signs and Sounds
>
> - If your customer has been fairly quiet and suddenly begins asking a lot of questions.
> - If your conversation picks up the pace or slows down significantly
> - Expressions like "Ah" or "Yup" or "Aha" can indicate your customer is ready to own.
> - Facial expressions like smiles and laughter are very strong signals that your customer wants what you are offering.

Think about it, if they are smiling and laughing what are they telling you? They are saying "I like you; I trust you. I believe you." Good time to try a test close, don't you think? A test close is a question you ask to see if they are ready to be closed. It's not the final close, but it certainly can lead to it.

My mother and father provide a good example of the importance of reading customers' buying signs and listening for buying sounds. Being a knowledgeable mechanic, my father insists on making all the car-buying decisions. In fact, he is so convinced that my mother gives away too much with her enthusiastic comments and excited statements, that he makes her promise she won't say a word until the sale is closed. This is difficult for a woman who is as expressive as my mother, but she tries, bless her heart, to keep calm when they are car shopping.

Even though she's to be commended for her efforts, mother lets out with little peeps, sighs, raised eyebrows and rounded eyes when she just loves a car. It's all dad can do to keep her silent until they are driving off the lot. Well, needless to say, car shopping with my parents is better than the best *I Love Lucy* comedy show. Here's dad marching around the lot looking under the hood, kicking the tires, giving all those nonverbal buying signs. And mother is beside him with her hand over her mouth and frowning so as not to give away her feelings of excitement. A good salesperson who takes the time to read the reactions of my parents would get enough information for a book on body language and verbal and nonverbal buying signs. The funny thing is, my father is giving just as many nonverbal buying signs as mother. He's just not aware of his body language give-aways.

So, looking for those signs, both verbal and nonverbal, lets you know where you're at in the sale. Be sure to pay attention to your own gut feeling.

Once you're aware of it, you may be surprised to realize that part of the thing called "gut feeling" is actually a result of reading nonverbal body clues.

If your customer asks for another demonstration of your product, or wants to know more details about warranties, those are very strong buying signs. Some salespeople lose patience at that point and look at that as wasting time. Think again! Would a person who wasn't interested in what you were offering want to take up any more of his or her time? Absolutely not! He or she would be as eager for you to leave as you would be to get out of there. If customers ask for you to demonstrate the features one more time, believe me, they're interested and you should be, too.

The following are some questions that prompt buying signals from your customers.

- Ask questions that require one of two positive responses. No matter what response they give you, what they've really given you is a buying sign.
  Ex: "Will we be training you or all of your staff on the new software?" Or, **"Would you prefer delivery on Monday or would Tuesday be better?"**

- Ask questions that encourage your customers to assume ownership.
  Ex: **"How many of your people will be using our copy machine on a daily basis?"**
- Sometimes you can prompt your customer to reveal buying signs by answering a question with another question.
  Ex: **Prospect:**   **"Do you have a mutual fund that is a little more conservative?"**
  Salesperson: **"Are your financial goals safety driven or return driven?"**
- Ask assumptive questions.
  Ex: **"Now, how do you spell your last name?"** Or, **"What is your correct mailing address?"**   Then answer with, **"Let me just jot that down on the paperwork."** Or perhaps, **"What is today's date?"** Then, **"Thanks, let me just jot that down on your form."**

A big challenge that I have been able to help salespeople overcome is realizing the fact that customers do not always think the same as they do.

> It is a mistake to try to think for the customer at the closing stage, so you must continue to attempt to close when you feel you've earned the right to ask for the order.

Just keep trying, even if your timing is off and you've tried to close at the wrong time, just keep closing. You'll soon get the hang of it, and everything will fall into place when you are able to read all the different things we have talked about in this book. Then you'll develop your own closing style through practice and success in perfecting the closes I'll teach you. You'll be able to close almost anytime, anywhere.

My point—until you have years of experience under your belt, you shouldn't wait for a perfect time to close. There is no perfect time to close. In fact, there is no time like the present. Close throughout the entire process and allow the final close to happen naturally if your customer indicates to you they are ready to own. Of course, that is the ideal situation, but most people need a little prompting to get them past their fears and concerns. That's okay. That's why they come to you as the trained expert on your product or service.

> Closing the sale is a predictable process as long as you truly believe that what you are selling is good for the customer.

Ask yourself this question: If they don't buy from you and own your product and service, have they made a mistake? You better say yes—make sure you have that type of belief in what you sell. If you truly believe in the benefits your product or service will bring to your clients, you'll know making that ownership decision will be the best thing they can do and it's your obligation to help them see that, too.

Where Do You Close?

If you can close at any time, you certainly don't have to be picky about where you close, either. The rules about closing are that there are no rules about closing.

If you are in your car, you'll realize you don't have to wait to get back to the office to close. Hand your customer the paperwork and a pen and ask them to jot down what they have already said they wanted on the form. Get them used to handling and seeing the agreement. Many selling situations have been closed on construction sites, at restaurants, on golf courses, or at parties. When I was in the fitness industry, I closed many sales on fitness machines. So, always be prepared and remember your ABCs. **ALWAYS BE CLOSING!**

The key is to be prepared. I'm sure you've heard the saying "Carpe Diem"—Seize the day! Well, salespeople need to seize the closing moment. When your customer is excited to own, let them own your offerings no matter where you are. **ALWAYS BE READY!**

In a traditional setting, it is a good idea to keep a copy of your agreement or paperwork right on top of your notepad. Some may tell you to keep it out of sight until you're ready to close. I disagree. Make it known in the very beginning that you have nothing to hide when it comes to your paperwork.

When you lift your notepad out of your briefcase, or simply carry a portfolio into the meeting, you'll be able to make notes on your paperwork as you work through the process. That way there is no nervousness on the part of the customer if you whip out paperwork at the last minute. That can be an uncomfortable transition to make. Don't risk having them think something like this: **"Oh no, this is it. Now I have to sign my life away!"**

Instead, they will just be authorizing a form they have agreed to let you take notes on and, to the customer, it is no big deal. They have already seen you take it out and they are accustomed to seeing you write on it. In fact, if you have been respectful and asked for their permission to take notes, they've already agreed to let you take out your paperwork and begin filling out the necessary forms for a smooth close.

An Effective Close Helps All Parties R.E.L.A.T.E.

It's now time to relate to the customer in a manner that evokes the final decision. Let me explain what I mean by **R.E.L.A.T.E.** When you relate well to your customers during an outstanding close, you

R einforce features and benefits and recap solutions.

E liminate customer doubts.

L eave your customers with a positive feeling about you and your product and service.

A cknowledge your customers by hearing them out.

T ake it to the next step by simply filling out the paperwork or acknowledging agreement of the sale.

E valuate and adjust your closing depending on customer responses and behavior.

When you **R.E.L.A.T.E.**, you are enabling every person involved to experience the benefits of owning your product. That is what is meant by a win/win situation. You know what, I really don't believe in a win/lose selling situation. If everybody doesn't walk away from the table a winner, nobody wins. If somebody feels slighted or taken advantage of, how eager do you think they'll be to do business with you again or send you referral business? Not very! So **R.E.L.A.T.E.** well to your customers and everybody will be rewarded with a win/win situation. Sales is a game, but in the game of selling there can be no losers. If the game of sales is played correctly, all players win.

Prepare Mentally and Physically for the Close

We've already talked about having all your paperwork ready, and that is certainly part of the physical preparation for closing. Other physical preparations to make your customer feel more comfortable can be moving your chairs closer or shifting the paperwork so you can both read it. Make your closes as memorable and comfortable as you did the rapport-building stage of your meeting. Be prepared to close on a physical and mental level. The best way to prepare mentally is to put yourself in your customer's place.

Ask yourself these questions, and you'll certainly be in a better mental frame for a comfortable close:

1. What will my customer feel like after they own my product or service?
2. What will I feel like after I close the sale?
3. Will I be able to walk away from the close knowing that everybody benefited?
4. Will my customers' experience be so positive they won't hesitate to refer business my way?

If all the answers to these questions are positive, you have closed the sale and remained customer-focused. You'll leave the door open for added opportunities, add-ons or up-sales with this particular customer; to build and deepen the relationship with them and all those they refer to you. What have you done? You've created a positive selling cycle. You've practiced the principles of investigative selling and have proven they work. Fantastic!

What Is the Importance and Impact of Testimonials During a Close?

Don't underestimate the power of a strong testimonial. There is nothing like one customer telling another all the positives about owning your product and service. Who understands better what that customer may be experiencing than one of their peers? When you get testimonials, you may want to consider doing so in different formats so you have covered all your bases. Let me explain a little further what I mean by different formats.

When you need an endorsement from a client, especially one whose name means something to your prospective customer, you may want to arrange ahead of time that you will be placing a call at approximately so and so time. Let your satisfied client know your plans and ask their permission to give them a call. If you have properly acknowledged their value, they should be more than happy to accommodate you. Then, when you are ready, simply pick up the phone, introduce the satisfied customer to your prospective customer and let them talk.

> You just sit and listen. Having satisfied customers is like having a little army of closers out there working in your behalf, and you don't even have to share the fee you'll earn with them!

In addition, you may want to have testimonial letters on hand to show your prospect. Make sure the testimonial letters you take are fairly current and mention the particular benefits that best fit your prospects' needs and wants. This will immediately get their attention. As a salesperson, I have found that a lot of clients have good intentions when you ask them for a testimonial. Unfortunately, they do not follow through. I suggest you write a letter on their letterhead and have it ready for them to approve. If it represents their feelings about you and your product and service, and they like you, they won't have a challenge going to bat for you.

Along with the letters, you may even want to have an audio cassette tape to play an enthusiastic testimonial from a client with similar needs and wants. If you decide to use the tape player, be sure your batteries are alive and well, and that your equipment is in working order. There's nothing more embarrassing than playing a testimonial tape that says nothing or sounds like the speaker is in slow gear.

Finally, you may occasionally want to leave your prospect with an audio or video cassette tape, especially if you are making a multiple call close. Whatever they can take with them to reinforce the points made will give them reason to allow you more time in the future. In this case, have testimonials that will travel on tape with your customers.

Be More Than Just An Order Taker

A good investigative salesperson does more than push paperwork or get okays on documents. In a perfect selling world, maybe all you need do is hand the customer your agreement and a pen, say "Here" and then collect the order. I hate to break it to you, but I've rarely had an ideal sale. Although, to me, that is what makes selling so much fun. It's a daily challenge, and I want everybody to win. In order to make sure this happens, I need to be more than just an order taker; I have to orchestrate the close. I have to do my homework and then ASK for the sale. Then I make arrangements for the next step—follow-up and servicing the customer, which we'll talk about in the next chapter.

> Good investigators understand that closing is not the end of the transaction, but rather the beginning of the relationship.

As committed as they were to attaining the business, they should be committed to remaining a concerned and caring representative through continued service and customer contact. Future business depends on current service and follow-up!

A Word of Advice When Closing

Before you close, you may want to use the test close. Remember, the test close is a question you ask when you see some buying signs. With a test close you investigate how close the buyer is to making a decision. A test close does one of two things:

1. It gives you agreement that they are ready to go ahead
2. It gives you the area of concern or real reason they don't want to go ahead.

There comes a time when you have to ask the closing question, so ask! Then SHUT UP. Why? You've got to wait for the customer to give you the go ahead or give you the real reason they won't go ahead. And, you've got to listen!

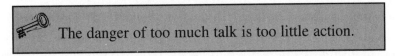

The danger of too much talk is too little action.

When you are talking you can't be listening to your customers' concerns. If you refuse to resist the temptation to talk, know that your income will be reduced proportionately to the time you spend talking. Moment by moment, as that clock ticks away on meaningless conversation, you get further and further from a successful close.

Let me give you the Final Closing Sequence, which summarizes the sales process and goes for the final close. You are in your final closing sequence when you have:

1. Summarized all the "yes" points.
2. Asked a final closing question.
3. Listened to their decision to go ahead, or their reasons why they won't go ahead.

If you've attended any seminars in the past, I'm sure you've heard it said that the first person to speak after an attempted close loses. A truer statement was never made.

> If you have done your job and asked a closing question SHUT UP and let the customer think. Don't be uncomfortable with a minute or two of silence.

I'm the first to admit that one whole minute without talking right after a close seems as though an eternity has passed. However, once you experience success, the next wait becomes that much easier until you are quite comfortable waiting for what you have earned—a positive response. Remember, when you shut up you're going to get the final "yes" or you'll hear the true area of concern and move forward to overcome it.

The first time I heard this SHUT UP theory, I was at a Tom Hopkins seminar. He first said, very gently, "Whenever you ask a final closing question…" Then he repeated it even softer, "Whenever you ask a final closing question…" Then he placed the microphone right up to his lips and yelled SHUT UP! It startled me so much that my knees hit the bottom of the table, but I never forgot his great advice. Now I know when to SHUT UP and close!

During my health and fitness sales career, I was involved in many corporate sales transactions. One day I was with an old timer in the insurance business. He owned his own insurance company, and I wanted him to send his entire corporation to my health clubs. He was a tough prospect, very savvy to selling techniques. But, I was determined to do what I did best, and that was to follow the proven fundamentals of great sales. I was attempting to close him using the predictable Ben Franklin, pros and cons method. Everybody and their uncle knows this close, including my customer who had actually studied with the great J. Douglas Edwards, one of the most knowledgeable sales trainers of his time. But that didn't deter me! I kept using the reliable, proven closing techniques and he kept saying: "Omar, you aren't going to use that old Ben Franklin close, are you?" When he asked that question, I said, "Well, it works for me!" Then I continued preparing for the close, and the customer played along thinking he would humor me. But still, he followed my lead. Before you know it, he looked down at his long list of reasons for ownership and his rather short one for reasons against owning my offering, and he paused. I used another technique I'm sure he recognized. I mirrored his behavior and also paused. There was silence! Total silence! Unending silence! Deafening silence! Silence for an entire seventeen minutes. Can you imagine? Seventeen whole minutes to set in front of a prospect and never say a word? I even excused myself and went to the bathroom during the heavy silence. Finally the prospect broke the silence, laughing and saying, "Ah kid, hand me your paperwork! I walked away with the order. My silence was my best selling tool!

Persuasive Closings Means Closing with Empathy Not Sympathy

There is a big difference between empathy and sympathy. Let me share with you a situation that will illustrate my point. You have finally been given permission to present to the new director of marketing, and when you get there all she can talk about is her busy schedule. Don't waste the precious time you have talking about how busy you are, too. Instead, acknowledge your understanding of her predicament; and, share with her the solutions your product and service can offer. That's empathy. You know how she feels, and that is why you are there—to help her become a better and more effective manager. When you first understand and then offer solutions, you've got the customer's attention.

You'll hear some salespeople say that you have to open the wound, remind the customer of his or her hurt, and then be the healer with the remedy. I disagree. Let me ask you, do you have to be reminded that you have a nagging headache or an upset stomach in order to get relief? Absolutely not! Don't waste your clients' time mulling over hurts or opening up old wounds. If you do, you may get them off on an irretrievable tangent. Instead, acknowledge their feelings and move on by offering immediate, emergency care. After all, don't you think they're more interested in being cared for than expressing their need for care? You bet they are!

Now You Must Master the Closes

I have written some great closes for you. 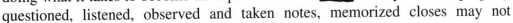 Commit yourself to doing what it takes to become an expert closer. If you have properly questioned, listened, observed and taken notes, memorized closes may not necessary. Great! However, you'll be even more prepared for knowing the concepts presented here. If you have practiced and mastered all the investigative principles, closing will simply be a matter of filling out a form or getting an agreement.

Master Closing Techniques

1.   The "Where Are You Now?" Close

You will probably hear someone say they're not really sure about going ahead. Remember, this objection is really only a smoke screen, and it is your job to uncover the real objection and move toward a successful close. Here's how you handle it. **"I understand how you feel. You know what, I don't want you to make a decision until you're 100 percent sure you are making a good choice. Just to let me know where we are at here, where are you now? Would you say you are about 80 percent sure of your decision to move ahead? (response) Let me ask you a question. What kind of reassurance would you need in order to feel 100 percent secure with your decision to move forward?"**

When they answer that last question, they'll be telling you exactly what they need to hear from you in order to go ahead. Isn't it great what investigative strategies can do for you?

2.   The Price Is Too High Close

When your prospective client says that the price is too high, you'll have to investigate to see if the real reason for not buying is that it costs too much or that they need to stall for more time. On large ticket items such as cars, homes, boats or even furniture, the price might really be the challenge. The following sequence of questions will enable you to get a handle on just what they're talking about. **"Let's put aside the money issue for a moment. What is your vision right now of where you want to be five years from now? (response) Okay, how important is it for you to achieve that goal? (response) How will achieving that goal change your quality of life? (response) Now let me ask you a very important question, John, how will saving and not spending the $2,500 affect your lifestyle? (response)**

If I understand you correctly, are you telling me it's more important to hold on to that money than it is to (state their wants that your product or service can answer)? (response) Level with me, John. What is this waiting going to do to your dreams? I thought so! When would you like to take delivery, Monday morning or would Wednesday evening suit your schedule better?"

Another method of approach when prospective clients say your product or service costs too much is simply to find out the exact dollar amount that's bothering them and then handle just that amount. Tom Hopkins teaches this quick, yet effective method for getting down to the final dollars in his seminars: **"In today's world most things do cost too much! Will you tell me, how much too much you feel it is?"**

Once they tell you the difference between where you are on the price and where they'd like to be, you can either suggest a lower-priced product of service, or take some time to build value so they can see that the price really isn't all that high.

3.   The Shop-Around Close

When the client tells you they want to shop around, they are stalling because they either don't believe something you said and want to verify it, or they think they can get it for less somewhere else. If your company has any sort of guarantee or return policy, this is when you use it to close. You should say, **"We have a written policy that states if for some reason you find a better investment, we will give you a full refund within 30 days. With this policy you win whether you keep the product or not. You can begin enjoying the benefits of the product today, yet still have the luxury of knowing if you find a better investment, we'll take care of you. So why not have the best of both worlds and go ahead now?"**

NOTE: I recommend using this close only as a last resort when they're ready to walk out the door without your product.

4.   The "Somebody Else's Shoes" Close
It never hurts to tell a hesitant customer about someone else you worked with. Tell them how the other person felt, what their needs were and what the resolution to the story was. If they went ahead, talk about how the client is now enjoying all the benefits of your offering because they didn't procrastinate but said yes that day. Or, you can tell a story of a customer who could have made a decision to own but chose to procrastinate. When they finally decided to buy, they missed out on months of enjoyment or the offering was in such demand the investment was much greater than they had originally planned.

5.   The Soda Pop/Candy Bar Close
This is an excellent close to use when price is definitely an issue. What you do is break down how much too much they feel the product and service is. Then compare it to some way they could make a small sacrifice to have the product, which is of much greater value. It is important to understand that you don't do this with the entire cost of the product, just with the amount they feel is over budget. You break it down together, to yearly, monthly, weekly, and even daily or hourly amounts if appropriate for your product or service. Then compare it to something ridiculous like the cost of a soda pop or a phone call. Do it in the form of a question. Your question might be something like this: **"Would you be willing to forego a soda pop a day to drive this beautiful car you've always dreamed of owning?"**

6.   I Need To Discuss This With My Spouse (Partner, Board, etc...)
I wanted to add this close because some salespeople do not qualify properly and have not discovered this objection by asking questions during the qualification period. If the prospect suddenly says, **"I really need to discuss it with my spouse."** You say, **"Is your spouse involved in the final decision?"** If they say "yes," you need to regroup and close on the opportunity to give another presentation—with all the decision-makers present.

7.   <u>The Paperwork Close</u>

This is used anytime in the sales process when you feel the client is ready to own your products or services. You simply move onto the paperwork and assume they're going ahead. If they don't stop you, you've closed another sale!

8. <u>The "If I Can Deliver, Are You Ready" Close</u>

This type of close can also be used to discover whether the objection is real or a smoke screen. Let me caution you though, if used on certain personality types or under emotionally-charged conditions, this may seem too pushy or manipulative. In essence, you're calling their bluff and trying to get them to show you their hand. Use it sparingly. Ex: The prospect says, **"I wish the carpet were in earth tones."** You come back with, **"If I could change the color of the carpet to just what you want, would you be prepared to authorize the agreement today?"**

This close will also smoke out any other objections the client may have about the product or service.

9. <u>The Third-Party Testimonial Close</u>

This type of close requires planning, recruiting, and schedule arranging, but it can be one of the most powerful closes. In a situation where your customer is still concerned about the return on his or her investment or your personal competence level, i.e. there may be doubt that you will serve them as well as he or she would like. **When you've thoroughly answered every objection, and the next one still crops up about the time you are moving toward the close, that is the time you suggest calling one of your most satisfied clients or your sales manager. Have them handle any unanswered questions regarding your ability to fulfill their needs. Of course, this needs to be planned ahead of time and requires a good deal of sensitivity on your part in order to avoid abusing your manager or customer's time. After the call has been made and your client has heard from someone else about the benefits of your product and service, then ask for the order.**

10. <u>The Take Away Close</u>

This is good to use with customers who like to make decisions on their own, ones who are internally motivated and determined not to be influenced by your persuasive techniques. Simply take away the opportunity. **Ex: "Mr. Howard, since you have been hesitant to own our offering, I'm sure you have reasons, and I wouldn't try to persuade you to do anything to convince you otherwise. Maybe you're not ready to make a decision. I'm curious what makes you so hesitant about going ahead today**?" Shut up and listen for an objection, then handle it. Remember, objections and concerns are good!

11. <u>The "I Want To Think It Over" Close</u>

This is probably Tom Hopkins' favorite close. That's because it's one of the most common stalls people use and the phraseology he's developed works so well in isolating the real final objection as the money. Here's what Tom suggests you say: **"I understand how you feel, Sam. Thinking it over makes a lot of sense. I'm sure you're not telling me this just to get rid of me. Just to clarify my thinking, what is it about this opportunity that you want to think over. Is it quality of the product? Is it the service I'll render? Is it the company? Please level with me, Sam, could your hesitation in any way be the financial aspects?"** The key here is to list all those things you know they've already agreed to and work your way down to the money. In 90 percent of sales, that is the real final objection. Once everyone admits that, you can reduce the money to the minimum amount and close the sale.

12. <u>Reduce It To the Minimum Close</u>

Take the total amount of time that your product or service is used and reduce the amount of money they're hesitating about to how much that is each year, month, week, day or even right down to the hour that they'll be owning and using it. In many cases, the amount reduces to something so minimal that they feel silly even objecting about it.

13. **?**   The "WHY" Close

My good friend and mentor, Dick Gardner, told me about this simple little close. It's an ideal example of an investigative technique. Children have cornered the market on this close for generations. It's called the "Why?" close. When your prospects give you an objection, simply say **"Why?"** You can say **"Really, why?"** Or, **"Why is that?"** The WHY close will help the prospect to elaborate on their area of concern and give a concrete objection to handle.

14.   The Alternative Of Choice Close

This type of close gives the customers two choices, either of which would mean they were moving ahead with the sale. So, if they say they'd prefer one to the other, you just make a note on your paperwork or laptop and assume they've decided to own your offering. **Ex: "Mr. Jones, will your company need two fax machines, or do you think your secretaries could share a machine?"**

15.   The Assumptive Close

An assumptive close is direct, a "that's no bull" sort of close that asks for the business. **"Mr. Buyer, you have agreed that your company needs our product, and I've shown you how to make the most return on your investment by handling your needs now, and still leaving an upgrade path for the future. After you've owned our computer for 120 days, I'm positive you'll discover the figures I've given you, today, to be conservative as to your actual savings."** (Hand the customer the paperwork and say "Here!")

16.   The Triplicate Close

This close is used when your product, service or money amounts have at least three different options or choices for the client. **Ex: "We have three sets of terms, Mr. Smith. It just depends on what works for you. The first is with payment in full, and we offer a 5 percent savings. The next is** designed for those who don't care for monthly investments. If that is the case, you can put 50 percent as an initial investment now and cover the balance on receipt. Or, we can schedule 1/3 initially and then monthly amounts after you've taken ownership. Which one of these terms best suits your needs?"

17.   The "If They Were Both Free" Close

This close is to be used when the client indicates they are going to go with the competition because they are less expensive. **Ex: "Let me ask you a question, Mr. Buyer. If these two products were both free, which one would you chose?"** If they choose your product, the close is simply a matter of pointing out to them that you're glad they have decided not to compromise quality for price. Then build value in your product!

18.   The Real Reason Close

This is when your client throws a question or brings up an objection and you throw it right back for a test close. **Ex:** Your client says, **"Do these Head skis come in a package that includes the boots and poles?"** You say, **"Are you interested in the best price on a package, or would you rather have the freedom to choose your own boots and poles?"** This gives you the latitude to find out if they are interested in price or the best opportunity.

19.   The Mistake & Correction Close

This is when you ask your client the date or their middle initial and repeat it back to them incorrectly. They then correct you. When they correct you, it means a "yes". **Ex: "Did you say you lived on East Main Street?"** The client says **"No, it's West Main."** You say, **"Great"** and begin writing or filling in your paperwork.

20. **Yes** The Summarization Close

In this close, you summarize all the benefits and features, build "yes" momentum and ask a final closing question. **Ex: "With your approval**

**right here, you will begin enjoying the benefits of being a member of this
health club and having the body you always dreamed of!"**

21. **$**   <u>The Value to the Customer Close</u>
This close is used on the customer whose concern is that the product or
service costs too much. Your challenge, as the salesperson, is to clearly show
them the return they'll be getting on their investment. In other words, how
much money will the customer make from owning your product or service?
During your investigation, you should be able to learn what the prospect's
customers are worth to him or her. What will they make on your product or
service? Then, determine how many more sales your prospect needs in order
for your product to pay for itself. Ask the prospect how many more
customers they will be able to attract by owning your offering. They have
then overcome their own "price" objection by telling you exactly when they
think the product will pay for itself.

22.   <u>The Competitive Edge Close</u>
Remember, when you're using the competitive edge close, do not bad-mouth
your competitor. Earn the right to give your presentation by pouring on the
professionalism.
   The Competitive Edge Close is done in four easy steps:
   1. Who are you currently using?
   2.   Are you happy with your present company?
   3. Were you the decision-maker when the decision was made to use
       (current company)?
   4. If "yes," ask them the benefits they received working with (current
       company). If "no," ask them if they are interested in increasing their
       BOTTOM LINE PROFITS or PRODUCTIVITY or (name their "hot
       button"). Earn the right to make your presentation.

   Will these closes work for you every time? Absolutely not! However,
think of how much improvement in your investigative sales performance you will
see if they were to work even 80 percent of the time. By becoming a strong closer,
you won't be wasting all your investigative efforts shooting from the hip; instead,

my goal is that you have the tools and understand the concepts. You'll be using all the things you've learned to benefit your customers, your company and yourself. Practicing and perfecting the closing principle will also strengthen your ability to answer objections, and will help you overcome the fear of rejection when you see that the worst that can happen is you get a "no" from the customer and leave with some referrals for another day.

Everybody loves doing what they're good at doing. Be an outstanding closer. The more you close, the more you'll continue to be a successful closer. Isn't that a positive chain of events?

Omar's Top Twelve Tips on How to Become a Strong Closer

1. Assume the prospect will buy. In other words, expect to make the sale, for most sales depend on this positive assurance in your attitude.
2. Build the sales momentum on minor agreements. Make it easier for the prospect to say "yes" than "no". Avoid phrases or statements in closing that will receive negative responses.
3. Don't get off the subject while closing. Many a sale has been lost because the prospect cooled off when the salesperson got off the subject.
4. Use statements that will induce buying action, such as: **"Let's go ahead with this!"** Or, **"Let's set it up this way."**
5. "He who hesitates is lost" Never hesitate when closing or the prospect will lose his or her confidence in you.
6. Back up your solutions and recommendations with great emotional reasons for buying. Keep investigating the prospect's wants, needs and issues. Return to the points that interest the prospect and tap those "hot buttons".
7. To clinch the sale, demonstrate proof, such as: usage figures, testimonial letters, case histories and proof stories.
8. Be alert for buying signals such as statements and questions by the prospect. A change in tone of voice can also be an indicator that they are ready to own your offering.
9. Don't oversell. It's almost as easy to talk yourself out of a sale as it is to talk yourself into one. Silence is necessary in some closing situations to enable the prospect to arrive at a decision.
10. In almost any selling endeavor, price enters in as the biggest objection. Prove that the price is right and you'll close many more sales. How much is a customer worth to them?

11. Be persistent in a tactful way. Successful salespeople credit almost 25 percent of their sales to making one more attempt to close just before leaving the prospect.
12. Simple and obvious—DON'T FORGET TO ASK FOR THE ORDER!

SUMMARY POINTS

- Closing begins immediately—before you even meet with the customer.
- Pay attention to customers' buying signs.
    - ✔ Laughter
    - ✔ Sudden interest and questions
    - ✔ Strong body language signals like head nodding and smiling.
    - ✔ Request for another demonstration
- It doesn't matter where or when you close.
- Effective closes help all parties **R.E.L.A.T.E.**

    R = reinforce features and benefits and recap solutions

    E = eliminate customer doubts

    L = leave your customers with positive feelings

    A = acknowledge your customers by hearing them out

    T = take it to the next step by simply filling out the paperwork

    E = evaluate and adjust your closings depending on customers' responses

- Benefit from the impact of testimonials to an effective close.
- Invest time in mastering the closing strategies of an investigative seller!
- Use Omar's Top Twelve Tips on How To Become a Strong Closer

INVESTIGATIVE PRINCIPLE #11
Be A 21st Century Salesperson

CLUE:

Get Prepared for the 21st Century.

"Keeping a little ahead of conditions is one of the secrets of business."
Charles M. Schwab

I couldn't leave this project without exposing you to 21st Century sales. Let me tell you, it's here right now, and if you aren't enjoying, yes enjoying, the perks of modern technology in your management, marketing and sales communications, you're missing out on a lot of business. Join today's superstars. When you finally give up all the paper-chasing methods of yesterday's business, you'll be amazed at how neat and convenient today's sales can be.

Let's see how up to date you are, shall we? Answer the following questions and then tally your score at the end to see how "with it" you really are.

1. Do you own a computer?
2. If you don't own a computer, do you at least know how to operate one fairly efficiently?
3. Do you have faxing capabilities, either by machine or through your computer?
4. Do you have a database of customers in your computer?
5. Do you have a computer database but still insist on keeping duplicate paper files?
6. Do you have a mobile phone?
7. Do you have a pager?
8. Are you familiar with electronic mail?

9. Can you browse the web and easily discover the information needed?
10. Do you research on the web?
11. Do you have a website?
12. Do you prospect on the web?
13. Do you and your company offer online sales and service?

SCORE:

13-10	Yes Answers = Power User Salesperson
9-6	Yes Answers = On the high end of this scale, you're getting there. On the low end, you're probably an average salesperson with average results.
5-0	Yes Answers = You work harder every day but never seem to get ahead. Someday they'll have to send in a forklift for all the piles of paperwork on your desk and those overflowing from your files.

I can hear some of you saying, I've prospered this long without all that fancy office equipment, so there is no reason for me to rock the boat now. What happens to people who think like that? Their income from sales matches their willingness to accept and learn new selling techniques and strategies.

Sales is an ever-changing business with limitless possibilities. The industry doesn't wait for you to get with the program. Your prospective customers won't overlook ignorant or stubborn salespeople who are unable or unwilling to provide high-tech services that bring higher quality products, increased profit shares and more efficient service . Your company doesn't make allowances for inefficient or nonproductive salespeople. The answer? Get acquainted with all the technological changes of the 21st Century and make yourself right at home.

Better Business Management Through Today's Technology

Wouldn't it be nice to see the last of that file cabinet that has been responsible for several stubbed toes, scraped knees, forever hidden folders, misfiled papers and layers and layers of last year's dust? You can store everything you have in one four-drawer file cabinet on a handful of small computer disks that can be easily reached, and files can be found instantly. No more cross-filing and referenced materials. Say goodbye to the hours upon hours of filing and searching, and hello to the extra income from adding those hours back into your sales schedule.

Design A Tailor-Made Database For Your Business

I'm not even going to say, if you have a computer... There is no question that you need to be computer literate or at least have support staff who can manage your business by computer. You should have a centralized storehouse of customer information on a convenient, easy-to-use database program. You'll have all your customers' and prospective customers' names, addresses, phone and fax numbers, last contact date, and special comments right at your fingertips. You'll know what they have purchased in the past and what they mentioned they would like for the future.

This will be one instance that you'll be a bit different from the investigator. There won't be a need for that writing tablet once you get back to your office and sit down in front of your computer. All your records will be on file on screen. You can categorize and itemize different fields of data, depending on your own individual needs. The best part about it is that you don't have to fear making mistakes and having to redo all the files. Hundreds of files can be deleted, added, transferred or renamed in a moment. In fact, you better be able to input information on the computer because the days of filing tons of paperwork will be obsolete.

The Efficiency of E-mail

I spoke to you earlier about e-mail but thought I would add just a bit in this section. The best thing about e-mail is speed. I personally think e-mail was created as a great time-management tool.

- When you have only a moment or two to get a message to a customer who has a reputation for keeping you on the phone for at least thirty minutes, use e-mail.
- When you are working at odd hours and don't wish to disturb the other person at that time, use e-mail.
- When there is no time to wait for that document to be mailed and a fax copy just isn't good enough, use e-mail.
- When you want to refer to what was said in a memo, use e-mail.

You can archive all your incoming and outgoing messages. And, when you want to solicit unbiased opinions about a product and service, or learn more information about a certain company, e-mail messages are the way to go.

How Can You Get An E-mail Account and What Will It Cost?

There are dozens of providers, but you have probably heard of America Online and Prodigy. These are very common online servers whose services are offered at a minimum charge per month. Most even have unlimited usage, like America Online. You do need to have a computer modem in order to send or receive e-mail. Most of the programs have directories and storage files so you can keep e-mail addresses within easy reach and you don't have to worry about where you put your address book. It's right there inside the program.

If you don't have an account already, you can sign up for Internet or register with one of the online providers and they'll begin billing you after thirty to forty-five days. I'm not sure how much each service charges their members, but many are under $20 per month.

Sending and Receiving E-mail

You can send FYI's to your customers through e-mail. You can read the morning's paper online. You can do your banking online. You can order office supplies and forms online. You can make travel arrangements online. There just isn't much that can't be done online. You absolutely can't remain stuck in yesterday's methods of selling. Just think, if it came down to the first salesperson to deliver the agreement and your competitor used a fax or e-mail while you used the traditional mail service, you stand to lose out on a lot of business.

Surfing the Internet or Browsing the Web

Not only is it a whole different world of office equipment and skills, but the language is unique as well.

> You can surf with no water, crawl with no legs, and browse without leaving your desk chair.

The web reminds me of something that was around a long time ago. Remember in the old movies when you see the outdoor markets where people strolled the narrow streets, stopping at this shop or that boutique for something special? Well, that's how the web is, except it is done electronically.

It's like an indoor market that your fingers travel through, stopping at this key or that to do a little bartering here and there. You may buy at one website, sell at another and offer service information at still a third. You can investigate at all of them. Visit the websites of your customers and you'll soon get a strong impression of their business philosophy, mission, targeted customers, vendors, services, budget, and almost anything else you might care to know. Looking at who's linked to your customers' websites, you will have a good idea of sister companies with whom they have established great relationships. You can also distinguish how many locations they have and the size of each. On many sites, you can even pull up annual reports that reveal financial commitments and resources. All you have to do is harvest the crop of information within your computer.

Now there are even some libraries that are online. They offer access to almost every magazine and newspaper within these libraries. You can access special events sponsored by the library, find out the hours they are opened and closed, and whether books you need to read are currently checked out by another. Phone books, corporate indexes and statistics are available and periodically updated on-line for your convenience. So, not only can you do away with those file cabinets, but you also never have to worry about losing a library book or spending your paycheck making copies from a magazine you need for a team project. You'll have more information than you know what to do with at your fingertips.

A 24-hour A Day Service

Whether you're prospecting, presenting, closing or following up a sale, you can do it all in a fraction of the time on the computer. Most of the time when people need your number or location, they go straight to your website instead of looking it up in the Yellow Pages or calling information.

You can also market your company or yourself through a specially designed website. One of the most interesting things about the web is that you get to see new ideas and inventions before the general public sees them; they have been on the web before hitting the market. Your website can deliver information, sell you, your product or your company. Sometimes you can even get the company to pitch in with the website design costs or your on-line fees.

One of the most difficult things about depending on only the on-line services to market your company and those of your clients, is that they need to be frequently updated and linked to relevant sites of your affiliates to expand your on-line possibilities. Sometimes putting your site in several locations helps the consumer to find it in one area where the other may have escaped his or her notice.

A word of caution, though, do a lot of your on-line work outside business hours. Why? Because while you are on-line it will keep a phone line tied up all the time. You don't want to lose a sale while you were trying to get another one.

> You may want to consider getting a dedicated phone line if you find yourself doing a lot of surfing or crawling on the Internet.

No matter who you hire to be your server (company that handles your account and produces the Internet software), make sure you have 24-hour a day, seven day a week accessibility to your website. It would be tragic if you couldn't investigate when the time was right.

Limit Yourself to Working On the Computer During Working Hours

There are so many challenging computer games out on the market today, make sure you don't get addicted and forget to do your sales work. It is so tempting to play games on the computer that it is easy to put off the work. I can tell you one thing, having worked so long and hard on this project, I can understand the temptation to just play for a while. I would suggest you make it a habit to use the computer for business during business hours. Maybe you are thinking, "Omar, games aren't for me. I'm just not a games sort of guy or gal." I'll tell you, those are famous last words. Don't count on it. All I'm saying is set some rules for yourself as you try to balance your business time with your personal time.

Combine the Old with the New

Don't get me wrong. I'm not encouraging you to discard all your old ways. All I'm saying is that you must start to make the transition of moving toward today's technology. If you are a cautious type of person, that transition may be rather slow and painful. If you are more of an impulsive salesperson, you will want the latest gadget on the market. I will admit, even having the program manager and time-management programs on my computer, I still write everything in my planner and keep a Rolodex of addresses and phone numbers on my desk.

For years we have been talking on the phone to clients across country and have done business with them for months before we actually even met with them. Now we find ourselves doing business with people for a long time, never having seen or heard them. We just constantly communicate on-line. When you think about it, that is pretty amazing.

> Well, if you haven't updated your technology, it's time you did. Make sure your office has all the tools you need to make yourself an efficient and successful salesperson. Learn what is out there today because tomorrow's technological capabilities may build from the knowledge you have of today's technology.

You'll find the last chapter on maintaining your enthusiasm is much easier to do when you are working your business the smart way and don't spend all your time shuffling paperwork. You'll have more time for yourself and, consequently, more enthusiasm for your sales career.

So let's move to that last chapter and see just how important a positive attitude and enthusiasm is to your sales performance.

SUMMARY POINTS

- Manage your business through today's technology.
- Design your database.
- Learn how to e-mail.
- Surf the internet and investigate prospective customers.
- Control your for-fun computer time; focus on work during working hours.
- Combine the old with the new.

INVESTIGATIVE PRINCIPLE #12
Maintain A Positive Attitude and High-Energy Enthusiasm

CLUE:

Being Positive and Enthusiastic is Contagious and Powerful

"If you aren't happy where you are, you'll never be happy where you ain't!"
Omar Periu

I left the topic of attitude and enthusiasm until the last chapter for a reason. If you have been diligently learning all the skills presented in this book and practicing those skills out in the field, by this time you are probably in desperate need of some encouragement. I never said sales would be easy. In fact, I think one of the most important skills that superstar salespeople learn is how to survive the down times. They have learned how to get up when people and situations beat them down. They have learned to deliver a presentation they have given over a hundred times as enthusiastically as they did the first time they spoke its message. Most of all, they have learned the value of maintaining a positive attitude.

Your first step is making the biggest sale ever, and that is selling yourself on wanting to change. You should feel about having a positive attitude like you do about your "American Express" card—don't leave home without it! Up to this point, your character has been a complete sum of the thoughts you think. Whether they are positive or negative—thoughts bring you results. Change your thoughts and you'll change your future.

Think of it this way. Your customers don't want to hear about your difficulties; they want you to listen to theirs. You see, your customers will begin to link you with whatever feelings you help to create in them during your meeting.

It is paramount that they link positive thoughts to doing business with you and your company.

I'm not saying you're not going to feel the fear of rejection or the sting of a "no" response after a well-executed presentation. You will, time and time again. What's important is not how much you feel those things, but how often you can say NEXT, forget about it, and move on to the next customer.

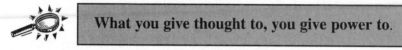

What you give thought to, you give power to.

Focusing on the negative only makes it stronger.

Interrupt Your Negative Patterns—Just Say NEXT!
Maybe you've tried this all before. It didn't work then, so you believe it won't work now! I'll let you in on a little secret. If you are thinking this, you are probably right.

What you believe to be true, usually is!

When your thoughts follow negative patterns, you are your own worst enemy. You are so busy filling your head with negative thoughts, there's not much room left for anything else. Thoughts precede actions, so take a strong, hard look at your self-talk. If nothing seems to go right for you, change the tapes you're playing in your head. Give yourself positive talk. Say what I say:

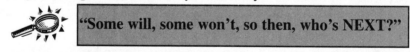

"Some will, some won't, so then, who's NEXT?"

One of the things I like to do while I'm running in the morning or the evening is let the positives come in and the negatives go by. This is how I do that. As I run, I actually hold my arms and hands at my sides. In a Karate-type motion, I move one hand one way and pretend I'm telling negatives to "go by," and I move the other hand in the opposite direction and say to the positives "come in." I feel great mentally and physically when I've finished a good run! Not only have I changed my physical self, but my mental self has been exercised as well.

In order to change, you have to make a choice to interrupt the negative. Stop the negative dead in its tracks!

✔ Don't read and read about how to make things better and yet still do nothing.

✔ Don't discuss with others who feel as badly as you how much you would like to change. Soon you look like a band of losers.

✔ Don't continue to promise your family you will change, then do the same old nothing you have been practicing since the beginning of time.

It's time to ACT!

Okay, you've made the decision to change. One of the first things you have to change is the manner in which you think. Remove the words "I Can't" from your vocabulary. You may choose not to, but I'll tell you right now—"I Can't" is unacceptable! If you think hesitantly, and use doubtful words and phrases like "I hope" or "I think" or "I wish," your mind will never buy into your new way of thinking. Speak with conviction. Replace those weak words with strong, positive ones like "I am," "I can" and "I believe!" When you speak them out loud, into the mirror, put emotion and belief into your voice. If you can't convince yourself the first time, repeat the affirmation again and again. Get stronger each time you say the words and phrases. Positive affirmations without belief and conviction are simply empty, meaningless words. What is worse, the words are followed by the same old actions that lead to nowhere.

> **Changed actions begin with changed beliefs; convictions spoken out loud with feeling and passion.**

Sometimes change is very difficult, and you must will yourself forward. Let me share with you a story about a young boy who did just that—willed himself forward. Every evening when this young boy had completed his chores on the farm, he would walk to his girlfriend's house to spend some time with her. Now, he could take the long way around the farms, which meant walking ten miles, but he wouldn't have had as much time to spend with her once he got there, and his exhaustion would have kept him from enjoying the visit. So one day he chose to take a short cut through the neighboring farm. Although it cut off miles and miles of walking, it came with its own set of challenges. You see, his neighbor raised cattle, and in order to get to his girlfriend's home, the young man had to walk through the pen of one of his prized bulls. This bull was a champion, bred strong, fast and determined.

One evening he decided to take that short cut! As the young man jumped the fence to the bull's pen, and got about half way across, he was surprised and somewhat apprehensive that he had not seen the bull. Surprised, that is, until he heard the raking of hoofs and the mad snorting of the bull coming right for him. There was no time for reasoning; he quickly turned and began to run like crazy. With each step he felt hot bull breath on the back of his neck! Now, I don't know how many of you have ever felt hot bull breath smack on the back of your neck, but it's terrifying! Snorting that sounds as loud and powerful as a train closing in on you, and you have nowhere to go!

During these few short moments, the young man was focused on just one goal—staying out of the reach of the bull's powerful horns. As he ran toward a tree in the corner of the pen, he knew his only chance to clear the horns of the bull was to jump for one of the branches with all his might. By the time he reached the tree he could actually feel droplets of bull slobber hitting his neck. No time left, he must jump NOW!

He looked at the limb he had in mind and jumped to an incredible height, stretching his arms out as far as they would go. But it was no use. His hands missed grasping the limb by inches. Just as he was about to give up hope, dropping from one branch to another, suddenly he knew he would win. On his way down he grabbed hold of the very bottom limb, barely staying out of reach of the crazed bull.

Why did I tell you this story? I love the lesson to be learned in the young man's dilemma. First of all, there are no short cuts! You must pay a price for success. I know many salespeople who climb that same tree everyday, grasping at anything they can get their hands on, only most of the time they aren't as lucky!

One good thing that the young man did was to will himself forward and stay focused on his goal.

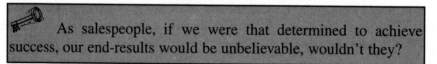

As salespeople, if we were that determined to achieve success, our end-results would be unbelievable, wouldn't they?

He also set his sights on a goal to reach one of the top branches, and although he missed it by mere inches, he caught another branch on his way down. That's what we need to do in sales, too. Set our sights on a goal that could be reachable if we stretched ourselves to the max, but have a bottom-line goal that must be achieved in case we fall short of the mark. Two goals—one at the top of the tree, and one that is your bottom-line "protect your backsides," necessary goal! What is your bottom-line? What can you absolutely NOT ACCEPT if you were not to achieve it?

No matter what, whether achieving your top or bottom-line goal, you must focus on a specific targeted goal and will yourself forward.

- You must take massive positive action in order to stay ahead of the pack.
- You must be committed to the sheer act of success in selling, not just survival.

Many salespeople survive in selling and hate what they do because they suffer the slings and arrows of disappointment, frustration and rejection and then they get up every morning and do the same thing all over again.

Every day in sales you create! You create greater opportunities, increased chances for success, or you create more suffering and dissatisfaction in your work. To be at the top, you've got to be faster, smarter, and more determined than the bull, and believe me, you will face the hot breath and snorting bulls in this industry. There will be some bullpens you'll have to cross, and you'll never make friends with them, but they'll teach you to be fast, quick-thinking and more focused than you ever dreamed possible. So welcome the bulls; they'll keep you at the top of your game!

Don't Make Doubt and Fear Your Invited Guests

Kick them out! This is the time for you to focus on what's best for **you**. It's easy to feel good when you don't have fear sitting on one shoulder and doubt on the other filling each ear with false statements and disbelief. In order for your heart and mind to accept what your voice is saying, you have to refuse to listen to the negative. Shut it off! Be deaf to the interference of negatives in your life. Even if you must physically move around, cover your ears and remove yourself from people talking negatively. That's what you must do in order to make room for the positive.

Positive and negative are not good roommates and, unfortunately, negative may be the stronger and more stubborn presence in your life right now. One of my students who was plagued with negative self-talk told me once that in order to get rid of it, he physically opened the door and booted it out. Belief cannot reside where there is doubt and fear. Do it! Open the door and kick out doubt and fear. You'll feel 100 percent better.

Now That You're In Control—What Do You Do Next?

If you have been consumed with the negative for a long time, positive attitude may be somewhat fleeting. You may have to work doubly hard to maintain a positive attitude. For some it may come easy, but for you it may be an ongoing struggle to remain positive for an extended period of time. It doesn't necessarily have to be this way, even if it has been in the past.

> You have a choice; a choice to let go of the past. Don't try to analyze or rationalize the negative. What for? Simply let go. It happened, it's over—NEXT!

Start A Personal Possibilities Program—Outline Your Expectations

In the past, you may have heard this referred to as taking a personal inventory. I prefer to think of it as a personal possibilities program. It helps me to focus on the positive again. I may identify my weaknesses, but what I'm really going to do is focus on my strengths and discover the possibilities those strengths offer me in both my personal and professional life. So can you!

Don't forget to be the investigator. Ask yourself positive questions just as you learned to ask your customers questions. What are your weaknesses? How are those affecting your beliefs and actions? What are your strengths? How can you use them to full advantage?

What steps must be taken to improve your weaknesses and make your strengths outstanding? When can you expect these changes to occur? Who else needs to be involved in the changing process?

These are just some of the questions you should be asking and answering in order to bring about effective change that INTERRUPTS the negative or breaks that negative pattern. Soon, instead of just saying NEXT to your negative thoughts, you'll have accomplished one positive and be welcoming the NEXT positive.

Let me caution you, though, about being overly concerned with your weaknesses when starting your personal possibilities program.

> 🔑 What you give attention to and focus on becomes your state of mind.

If you feed the weaknesses and starve your strengths, you'll become mentally defeated in the process. All you have to do is simply recognize what needs to be changed, take action, then say NEXT. Don't dwell on how badly you did this or how you wish you hadn't done that. Why? In the process you are giving a lot of thought to the negative. Instead, look forward to all the fun things you will learn while turning your weaknesses into your strengths.

You Must Be Ready for Change

Change is not an overnight process and there are no shortcuts. It can be temporarily painful, but the alternative is no change at all, right? I guess that's okay if you like where you are at right now. If you're looking to become the best you can be, however, you have to face life's constant changes and be willing to change right along with it.

One of the companies I train has a great sales manager by the name of Helene. She enrolls all new sales representatives in a two-week training program. While they're training, they are all pumped up and excited to sell. She knows that the rejection will hit once they're out in the real world, no matter how hard she tries to warn them. She also knows some will take the negative route, and destroy their chances of success before they even get started. That's why she has them write down the reasons why they chose to work for her company. Another thing she prides herself on is keeping an open line of communication in order to talk it out when her salespeople get down.

Throughout her years of managing people, she has discovered some universal truths. One of those is that you can always find reasons to quit or give up, but if those reasons are nipped in the bud by mentoring or a buddy system, you have a greater chance to move forward in the sales industry. If one person quits it can become a disease within the company, so she makes it her responsibility to continually sell her salespeople on the company. How? She keeps success stories or testimonials from highly successful company people.

Don't Join the Easy Crowd

There is some truth in what most of our parents used to tell us about the fact that we become like those with whom we spend time. A friend once told me that she visited an art gallery in Europe and stood before the Greek statute of Apollo. Apollo, of course, is the model of physical perfection. She shared with me an interesting realization she had as she stood before this magnificent statute. Everybody who stood before the statute for any length of time began to straighten their backs, pull their shoulders back, stand taller and adopt a more powerful presence.

If that is true, and a still, quiet statute can have that affect on us, just think of the influence a strong, powerful and productive mentor could have on your sales career! That's why I am constantly saying to read books; listen and look at tapes; get pumped up in the morning and it will motivate you to stay that way all day. Get in high gear to produce more than yesterday, the day before, and the day before that. Be a lean, mean selling machine!

> We are constantly selling. Either we sell the individuals and companies on getting involved with us, or they sell us on why they shouldn't get involved.

Another tool my friend has found invaluable is practicing the buddy system. She makes sure new salespeople have a buddy they can work with to help them vent and still remain positive. Because of her knowledge of managing people and her self-mastery, she has created an incredibly positive working environment where her salespeople look forward to contributing their highest achievements for a united effort toward common company goals. If you come from a negative base in her company, you're either going to change or leave. With her reputation, I can tell you most of her salespeople decide on change as the better option.

If the process of change for you seems endless and the problems insurmountable, you have to take it one simple step at a time and reward yourself for each small victory. Today is just one more step toward happiness and, in fact, you'll be happier in the process of change because you are achieving and improving on your road toward your final destination. Each day brings you one step closer to a better you. In reality, it's all those steps that build character, develop decision-making capabilities and strengthen your belief system. It's a day-by-day learning about self!

> The great thing about being so positive is the immediate improvement it has on your sales performance.

Your positive nature will make you a people magnet. Everybody wants to be around "up" people who know where they are going and see a lot of people joining the crusade. I'm sure you've met people whom you felt were movers and shakers, right? The vibrations they create are quite powerful, and so are the people.

Become A Student Of Positive—Investigate Success

Not only will you become a student of change and improvement in yourself, but you should also be investigating what makes successful people so successful. Find a mentor. Observe his or her behavior. Listen to their speech. Imagine what it would feel like to be just like them. Believe that you can be as successful or even more successful than your mentor.

Now is the time to be fearless. Do what I did when I first met Tom Murphy. Walk right up to your chosen mentor, introduce yourself and, if possible, ask to take him or her out for coffee or lunch in order to discover how you can do what they did. In Chapter Three we devoted a lot of time to learning how to become an active listener and an effective observer. I strongly recommend you re-read that chapter before you have lunch with your mentor. Don't be afraid! You'll be surprised at how many successful people are more than willing to share their stories with an eager listener.

One of the most successful network marketing professionals I know confided in me that she even taped her mentors. Every time she questioned what her mentor would do, she simply played back the tape and recaptured all the excitement and thrill of their first meeting. What a great idea! If you choose not to tape, be sure to take notes as you listen. Listen with attention to the similarities between you and your mentor. Perhaps a similarity in business philosophy or a like personality can encourage you to believe you can be just as successful. Make sure that your chosen mentor has a story with which you can relate. Most of all, leave the meeting saying, "I can do that! I can do that and even do it better!"

Take A Visualization Vacation

From adolescents on through our adult years, we are discouraged from dreaming. As small children, we were allowed to pretend and dream. Then, about the time we could have been taught to turn our dreams into realities, we were told to stop dreaming all together. What a shame! Dreaming can be very effective in achieving success. Here's how it works. First of all, stop thinking that dreaming is an idle pastime, it's not. Some of the most creative, successful and brilliant people in our country dreamed their way into our history books: Einstein, Edison, Franklin, Lincoln, Kennedy, King, Sojourner Truth and Eleanor Roosevelt. Their dreams were put down by many and their ways were difficult, but they continued to hold onto their dreams and they continued on to achieve greatness.

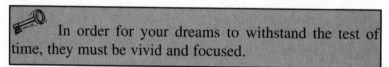

In order for your dreams to withstand the test of time, they must be vivid and focused.

One of the things I was taught years ago was to picture my dreams on a screen. I called it my dream screen. I would place all my dreams on the screen and make an incredible movie of them. By being able to clearly picture myself having my dreams, I was able to take the steps necessary to set my dreams into action. I fed them, and they became strong.

Right from the very beginning, I had higher standards than the average salesperson. My dreams were bigger, grander, easier to criticize. So I learned to keep them to myself at first, until my confidence level and belief could support them. Soon others began to believe what they saw me believe in so strongly. As I spoke of what I would accomplish and when I expected to have it happen, my friends and family would share my dream, feeding it a double portion of belief and desire. WOW! Talk about incredible activity in the dreams department. It was like, from my lips to God's ears.

Act On Your Dreams and Make Them Real

Once I began to believe in myself and others believed in my abilities to succeed, my dreams began to look real. It is a strange occurrence, but positive attracts positive. When I made a plan of action and began to see results, the negative people in my life just sort of fell by the wayside and achievers came forward to take their place.

An important part about a plan of action is to complete your cycles. Once you start on the road to achievement, let nothing distract you from your focus.

Become results oriented.

Make it an all or nothing endeavor. Don't **try—DO!** If the process becomes too difficult to maintain, you probably haven't broken your goals down into small enough steps, your belief needs to be strengthened before you attempt such a large undertaking. Don't give up; just step back and form a new plan.

Count On Courage—Be A Calculated Risk-Taker

Today's risky achievements are tomorrow's easy tasks. A little further in this chapter, we'll talk about the advantages of looking back on your achievements and renewing all those positive feelings of accomplishment you had at the time you reached your goals. First, however, we have to talk about goal-setting.

Picture and Pursue Your Goals with a Burning Desire

We've talked about picturing your dreams with detailed imagination. Now, you have to turn those dreams into achievable goals. Stay positive. Keep believing in yourself. Say "I can" instead of "I'll try!" It takes a lot of hard work, and if it doesn't you haven't set your goals high enough. Even though it's difficult, the victories are so much sweeter when you realize all the hard work that went into their achievement.

You will probably find others who will give you support and encouragement, but expect to accomplish your success on your own. Others can contribute, but you'll be the one to make it happen, and that's the way it should be. If not, you couldn't take full credit for your success, could you? Whether this is the first goal you have ever written (all goals should be in writing), or one of many, plan its achievement in detail. Write down the goal, the steps it will take to achieve it, the way you will celebrate your success, the expectations you have when you attain your goal, and how others will benefit from your goal as well.

If your spouse or significant other also stands to gain by your achieved goal, involve them in the process. Make it a shared venture. Two people working on a goal gets the job done that much sooner. Have check marks in your weekly planner and mark them up with small accomplishments! Then, you can always look back and see where you stand on achieving that goal.

After you have written down the goal, make sure you have listed the gradient steps you'll take to arrive at your destination. Each step can be a small goal in itself, with a mini celebration afterwards. Whatever keeps you on track and focused on its achievement, do it! One of the things I find most encouraging is to keep a journal of my successfully reached goals.

Tom Murphy was the one who shared this little gem with me, and it is incredibly effective. If I have lost the momentum of my goal, or my focus is weakened, I simply turn to my goals' journal and look back on all the ones I have previously achieved. It is a great mental boost. *"Without a goal, you are like a vessel without a sail. You are drifting. You will drift in the ocean of life! But, with a sale and a rudder, you will find the winds to take you to your planned destination!"* Omar Periu

Purpose Gets You Through the Tough Times

Give yourself great reasons to stay motivated: children, parents, friends, spouse, etc. Share your dreams with them; make them an important part of your achievement. Experience pleasure from giving. The road to achievement can be long and difficult; you'll need their participation and encouragement in order to be your best and find true happiness.

The real happiness is in achieving the goals. It makes you a stronger person, and you'll appreciate the strengthened character and heightened resolve you feel after the achievement of each goal. Some believe in meditation upon their goals. I choose prayer as my form of meditation. I pray daily, and share my goals with God. I must admit, He certainly hears my prayers and answers them appropriately. I'm often amazed at the unexplainable events that take place when I begin to meditate or pray for the positive achievement of my goals. That is when things really begin to happen!

Maintain a Focused State and Create More Momentum

Once you have a plan, stick to it, work it, complete it! Quite frankly, it takes a lot of self-discipline to stick to a goal that pushes you to the max and makes you stretch to achieve it. It's a sacrifice. Think of it this way—sacrifice a little today and gain a lot tomorrow. Sacrifice a lot today and gain a lot tomorrow.

Acting as if you have achieved your goal puts you one step closer to doing so.

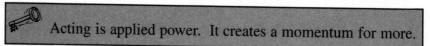

Acting is applied power. It creates a momentum for more.

One goal just whets your appetite. More knowledge, more happiness, more love, more recognition, more self-confidence, more money, more, more, more... I once heard that an ongoing, nagging dissatisfaction for more creates momentum, and I believe that to be true. Once you have achieved, you'll be satisfied with nothing less than more achievement. Once you taste the victory of accomplishment, the next day will bring with it a hunger for more.

You Must Have Purpose In Your Life

Discover what personally motivates you to take massive action. For me, I was sick of sitting inside my 220 square foot apartment and looking out the window at successful people walking into the restaurant across the street, sporting the happiness and self-confidence that success provides. They drove better cars than I did, wore better clothes and jewelry than I had, and they were major players in the success game where I was merely a part-time spectator.

Then I realized what motivated me, but there was more than just motivation. There were rules, laws and fundamentals that you must master to become successful. Sure, you can still get to the top if you don't know the fundamentals, but you won't stay there. And, when you crash and burn, it will be next to impossible to repeat your success. After all, it's difficult to duplicate success when you aren't aware of what creates it.

Many people think it's how much money you can make that determines your success. It's not about making money, but rather making yourself valuable to others.

Wealth doesn't always create value, but value almost always creates wealth.

Today, my number one motivation is to take care of my family. My goals involving their care touch my heart and soul and fire me up more than any other goal I've ever had.

Actually the hunger for greater accomplishments begins before you've reached the peak of the goal being worked on today, so you have to guard yourself against something that is a killer to accomplishment. Don't jump from one thing to another without having completed a cycle. Start out with small successes and build toward larger ones. But, whether small or large—complete your cycles. If all your achievements are almost done, you're still only hoping for success. See your tasks all the way through before jumping on the bandwagon of another exciting achievement.

Remember to Take Massive Action Today—RAMO!

What's Ramo? That's what I do to pump myself up and talk myself into doing what it takes every day to become more successful and maintain the success I have. Where did I get Ramo? It's Omar spelled backwards. It's part of my positive self-talk, and I use it to achieve self-mastery. Remember that self-mastery concept? It begins with your spirit, then your thought and finally your action. Continue to grow in all and you will experience the greatness of total self-mastery.

> Run toward what you want—not away from what you don't want! See the difference in thinking? Go full steam ahead creating opportunities; get the activity going! **Discover what personally motivates you to take massive action.**

All This Activity Takes Enthusiasm and Energy

It can be stressful, exciting, eventful, creative, fun and crazy, and above all it can be a physical drain. You won't notice it at first because you'll be too excited about all the newness and positive results. It's like having a rush of adrenaline, when it subsides you can experience a letdown. The best way to remain emotionally and physically stable is to be fit.

Different people express their enthusiasm in different ways, and some don't express it at all. When you think about it, we are taught from childhood to suppress our natural enthusiasm. What is it that we hear parents say to their kids every day "Calm down!" "Don't get so excited!" It's not that adults don't want to be enthusiastic, but many have just forgotten how to show their enthusiasm. They really don't know what enthusiasm is, so they act excited, but excitement isn't really enthusiasm. Or, they act zealous, but most of the time they simply succeed in annoying the people they're around instead of creating a contagious enthusiasm. What is enthusiasm, anyway?

What Is Enthusiasm and How Do You Get it?

- Enthusiasm is believing you have GOLD to offer to others, and then offering it as though you are giving them the opportunity to become richer in spirit and material gains than their wildest dreams.

- Enthusiasm lasts forever, it isn't just a passing parade that interrupts the ho-hum of your life.
- Enthusiasm is the inner inspiration that makes you look forward to getting up in the morning and the motivation that keeps you up at night.
- Enthusiasm is what gives you confidence and makes your customers trust in you and your offering.
- Enthusiasm is reflected in everything you do and say!

How do you get enthusiasm? You get it by being knowledgeable, sincere, courageous and faithful. You get enthusiasm by belief in yourself and your product or service. You get enthusiasm by being unafraid to express your true feelings and watching others as they catch your contagious feelings about your offering. You get enthusiasm by being as interested in your customers as you are in yourself.

Enthusiasm is the energy that blasts you to greater heights of success and makes you a winner. Doesn't everybody like to do business with a winner? Of course they do! You don't acquire more enthusiasm because you make the sale; you make the sale because you were more enthusiastic than the previous salesperson. When customers see your happiness and prosperity, they want the same for themselves and their companies. After all, emotions play a much more powerful role in selling than reason! Think good thoughts!

Don't Forget

Remember, your character, up to this point, is the complete summation of the thoughts you think. Positive thoughts equal positive results. Change your thoughts and you'll change your future!

Using the techniques in this book will help you keep your positive mental attitude and enthusiasm. Your sales will go up every month, making you look forward to every day!

Seven Disciplines Required to Maintain the Momentum of Enthusiasm

1. Always act with purpose! You will succeed in maintaining your enthusiasm if you learn from every human experience.
2. Know that you create and are totally responsible for your own experiences.

This empowers you to maintain your enthusiasm and not let anyone steal or diminish it.

3. Always stretch yourself to the limit, and commit to do something beyond what you believe your present capabilities to be. Be enthusiastic about your positive results.

4. Don't wait for perfection, do what you know to do today and continue developing your knowledge for tomorrow. With more knowledge comes more enthusiasm.

5. Be true to yourself! Be sure that your daily actions match your beliefs, and let nothing stand in the way of expressing those beliefs with great enthusiasm.

6. Let your enthusiasm create results that are desirable and work for yourself and others.

7. Deliver what you promise to yourself and others. Walk your talk!

Being the best person you can be isn't easy, and it takes a lot of help from those you love. Like I said before, find your motivation. If your parents are your motivation, make sure that your enthusiasm is expressed through the things that you do for them. My parents do happen to be my main motivators. When I treat them to a vacation, I enthusiastically make sure they are treated like royalty. They fly first class, stay in the best hotels and eat at the best restaurants. My wife, Helen, also motivates me, and it is my desire to enthusiastically show her how important she is to me.

It wasn't always that way. I must admit, when Helen and I were planning our wedding, my concerns were on the financial commitment we were making to the wedding. My focus was too practical. Helen wanted to fulfill a dream, one her father had built for her since childhood. As soon as I realized Helen's disappointment on my economic focus, I made up my mind that she would have her dream wedding. And, I will say, I'd do it all over again to see the joy on her face at our wedding. Every time we show our wedding video to family or friends, I see Helen deliver this wonderful thank you at the end. With a tear in her eye and a shaky voice, she says "I'd like to thank Omar for making my dreams come true." Wow, what enthusiasm she had, and what enthusiasm it created in me. Not the backslapping, loud sound of over-zealousness. Just a heartfelt love that expressed her feelings. Enthusiasm—it's the stuff that memories are made of!

Become an Athlete

As much of an emotional thing that enthusiasm is made of, it's also affected by the physical. Stay focused! Be disciplined. Be strong mentally and physically.

> It is a well-known fact that one discipline leads to another. Did you know that one addiction leads to another as well?

You can establish an addiction to something that would otherwise be good for you and turn it into a hindrance in your overall success. I've known people to do this with exercise, education, work, entertainment and eating. The key is to keep a balanced life.

Do you know someone who turned work into a way of life? Did it benefit them or their family? Chances are it split them wide open because they sacrificed personal relationships for business. Not good! I'm sure we've all met people who also saved money to the point that they forgot how to have a good time. Although saving money is good, if you refuse yourself the slightest bit of enjoyment, then you're out of balance and probably not experiencing the happiness you deserve.

Athletes learn early the importance of balance. If they overdo the eating and sacrifice their speed for strength, they are out of balance and probably out of contention. If the athlete is overly focused on training at the expense of having a bit of fun, when it comes time to compete, he or she will be mentally low and ill prepared for a win. You have to strike a happy medium.

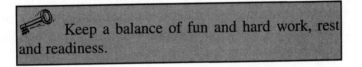

Keep a balance of fun and hard work, rest and readiness.

Whatever you do, enjoy the process because today is all you've got. Don't put off your happiness until you have saved $5,000, until you are married, until you are promoted to sales manager. If you postpone your happiness, you'll find it increasingly difficult to make yourself work toward achieving those goals. Take a look in the mirror and like the person you've become because of your achievements. You'll discover that goals are really secondary. Achievement is frosting on the cake of character building.

Have A Spirit of Thanksgiving for Your Success

Want is good unless the wanting becomes so strong it consumes you. Enjoying the process of achievement means liking who you are today while looking forward to what you will become tomorrow. Appreciate what you have and be happy with where you are right now. That doesn't have to mean you give up on your improvement plan, but look at your accomplishments of today.

Most of all, realize that you didn't achieve it alone. Whatever your beliefs, give thanks for the help you get along the way. I thank God! He has given me the knowledge and ability to teach and mentor. I thank others who have contributed to my success. I never forget where I came from and where I need to go in order to keep the satisfaction of accomplishment fresh and young.

Appreciation of what has been given to you doesn't mean just an expression of thankful words. What it is really about is giving back:

- ✔ Give to your community.
- ✔ Give to the children who desperately need your guidance.
- ✔ Give to your neighbors, family and friends.
- ✔ Give to your spouse.
- ✔ Give to your church, your city, your profession.

If you are stingy when it comes to giving, you'll be a stingy receiver as well.

Stay humble when you look at how far you've come. When you reach the top in your company or in your field of expertise, help others who could benefit from your experiences. Don't wait for them to ask for your help, but offer it in a way that makes it seem like it was their idea. Advise as though you are simply reminding them of what they are capable of achieving. Listen to their concerns and share with them your story of success with humility and a giving spirit. Who knows, maybe you'll be sharing this book with another who needs to hear the message of success!

You are the only one who can make it happen. God gives you the ingredients. You must make the bread. Pay the price to be the best. I wish you great success!

Success Is In the Moment—Make Every Moment Count!

SUMMARY POINTS

- Interrupt the negative patterns—just say NEXT!
- Make a commitment to change.
- Design a personal possibilities program for yourself.
- Become a student of success.
- Maintain a focused state—become results-oriented.
- Dream about your future with a burning passion.
- Set goals and plan for their achievement.
- Visualize and meditate on your success.
- Stay mentally and physically fit.
- Enjoy the process of achievement and the person you've become.
- Remain humble and maintain a thankful spirit.

GLOSSARY

A

Active Listening

Clarifying and confirming the message and responding by making eye contact, observing body language and expressing verbal and nonverbal agreement or opposition.

Activity Goals

Desired accomplishments that are measured by the successful completion of the ongoing behaviors needed to reach a pre-determined destination.

Alternate of Choice Question

These types of questions offer your customers a choice to move forward, or advance the sale to a positive conclusion, where everybody benefits. There is no bad choice.

Alternative of Choice Close

This close gives the customer two choices, either of which would indicate they are moving ahead with the sale.

Amiable Behavior

Focused on relationships; loyal and supportive-attentive and sensitive.

Analytical Behavior

Task-oriented perfectionists who love facts and figures.

Assumptive Close

Direct close that simply asks for the business.

Auditory Learners

These people relate to the world through the way things sound.

C

Close

The salesperson asks for the order. It's not the end of the transaction, but rather the beginning of the relationship.

Close-Ended Questions

Questions that require yes/no, or one-word responses.

Competitive Edge Close

Letting your customers know what you can do better than competitors, without bad-mouthing them.

COP Questions

Stands for <u>C</u>onfirmation <u>O</u>f the <u>P</u>ositive. When customers answer these questions, they are already seeing themselves as the owners of your offering.

D

Delegate

You do this by assigning tasks to others when possible so that you are given more time to plan, prospect and follow-up.

Driver Behavior

Direct, dominant and controlling person who talks and thinks on his or her feet.

E

End-Result Goals

Accomplishments that are measured by the success or failure of reaching your final destination.

Expressive Behavior

Interactive conversationalist; friendly and talkative; spontaneous and intuitive

F

FOCUSED

<u>F</u>eedback, <u>O</u>bserve, <u>C</u>ontrol, <u>U</u>se gestures, <u>S</u>tructure thoughts, <u>E</u>liminate distractions and <u>D</u>on't interrupt.

I

I Need To Discuss This With My Spouse Close

This is usually what happens when the salesperson has failed to properly qualify for the decision-maker.

I Want To Think It Over Close

This is the most common way for customers to stall before the close. It usually works down to the objection being a money matter.

If I Can Deliver, Are You Ready Close

A question used to determine whether the objection is real or only a smoke screen.

If They Were Both Free Close

Used when the client indicates they are going with your competition because they are less expensive.

Investigative Selling

Adopting the character of a great investigator by asking questions and gathering facts, listening, observing, taking notes, finding total solutions, closing and practicing great follow-up.

Itch Cycle

The customers' buying cycle that lets you know the best time to approach them on owning a new model or upgraded version of the one they currently own.

K

Kinesthetic Learners

These people relate to the world through touching and feeling.

Know It All Questions   (Sharp Angle Questions) Great questions that allow the customer to make a request that you know you can meet. Like a ricochet question that asks for the sale.

M

Matching and Mirroring   The process of reflecting the image of what will make your customers most comfortable. Almost like playing copy cat to their speech, behavior and movements.

**Mistake &
Correction Close**   When you ask your client the date or their middle initial and repeat it back to them incorrectly. When they correct you, it means a "Yes."

N

Nonverbal Language   Messages sent through expressions, sounds that are not words and particular behaviors or body movements that may indicate feelings, beliefs or emotions.

O

Objection   Statements from customers who want or need to know more information about you, your company or your product and service. Think of objections as opportunities and learn to welcome them.

Open-Ended Questions   These are questions that direct the conversation. They are your who, what, where, when, why and how questions. They give you a lot of qualifying information.

P

Paperwork Close

The salesperson moves to the paperwork when he or she feels ready to close.

Personal Formula for Success

The number of activities plus the number of contacts equals the number of appointments/presentations, which equals closed sales.

Personal Possibilities Program

Identifying your own personal strengths and weaknesses. Some refer to it as taking a personal inventory.

Poise

The salesperson's professional image and the manner in which he or she carries him/herself. It is your personal presentation.

Presentation

Your opportunity to position yourself and persuade your customers to see, hear, touch and believe in the superiority of your product and service.

Problem-Seeking Questions

These questions specifically seek to uncover problems. This type can be more difficult to word because many are spontaneous.

Prospecting

What salespeople do to generate business, finding people who will benefit from their products and services and then convincing them to own. Building your business by calling on people. It is a consistent and methodical search for clients.

Psycho-Cybernetics

The study of habits developed by Dr. Maxwell Maltz. His theory states that it takes 21 days of changed behavior to make or break a habit. The word "Cybernetics" comes from the greek word which literally means "The Steersman." Servo-mechanisms are so constructed that they automatically "serve" their way to a goal, target or answer. Psycho is derived from the word "Psychology," which means the study of the mind. Combine these two words and you have the study of how the mind serves to achieve your goals.

Q

Qualify

A step-by-step process of discovering information about your customer by asking excellent questions and practicing precise listening. Effective qualifying empowers you with knowing the needs and wants of your customers.

Qualifying for the "Highest Value"

If you have a customer who needs one type of product or service you offer, but you realize their true needs are those which your deluxe product or upgraded service package provides, you owe it to your customer and yourself to meet their needs. Don't just take the easy sale.

R

Rapport Building

Establish effective, long-lasting relationships with your customers by focusing on their needs, wants and issues.

Real Reason Close	When the customer throws a question or brings up an objection and you throw it right back for a test close.
Reduce It To The Minimum Close	Take the total amount of time that your product or service is used and reduce the amount of money they're hesitating about to how much that equates to per year, month, day and hour.
Referrals	Satisfied customers offering names of individuals or companies who can also benefit from your product and/or service.
Ricochet Questions	These are questions you ask in response to questions you hear from others. They allow you to discover exactly what the customer wants or what their concerns are.

S

Scratch Relief	If your investigations show that most of the company's consumers buy again every 18 months, you'll want to start tickling that itch a month or two before your past client has realized his or her need to scratch.
Selling Zone	The place where you are selling at your highest peak.
Shop-Around Close	The customers think they can get it for less somewhere else, so the salesperson encourages them to shop around. Then they ask the customer to come back and give them the opportunity to compete with their newly found price, terms or conditions.

Soda Pop/
Candy Bar Close

Use when price is definitely the issue, to break down just how much too much the customer believes your offering is.

Solution Questions

Great attention-getting tools. They lead the salesperson to solutions to customers' specific concerns.

Somebody Else's Shoes

Sharing what someone else did who felt the same way as this particular customer feels in this particular closing situation.

STP Questions

(Seeking The Positive) Questions that continuously solicit positive responses, or "Yeses" from the customer. Simple little "agree with me" phrases.

Summarization Close

The salesperson summarizes all the benefits and features, building "Yes" momentum.

T

Test Close

A question you ask to investigate how the buyer feels about your offering at this time.

The Price Is Too
High Close

If price is the issue, the salesperson must rationalize the product or service by reducing the money amounts to the minimum. Or, the salesperson must pour on the value to illustrate the worth of their offering.

Third-Party
Testimonial Close

An outside party is solicited to verify the truth of what you say or establish your credibility.

Triplicate Close	When your product, service or money amounts have at least three different options or choices for the client.
Two (2) To One (1) Ratio Recipe	Whenever you are in the selling sequence, ask two (2) personal questions to one (1) business related question in order to build rapport.

V

Value To the Customer Close	When the customer says it costs too much, you clearly show them the return they'll be getting on their investment.
Visual Learners	Those who are focused on images--what they can see is what they value most.
Visualization	Dreaming with vivid and specific mental pictures that help you turn your wants into realities.

W

Where Are You Now Close	A question that asks the customers what it will take for them to move forward with their decision to own.
Why Close	When your prospect gives you an objection, you simply say "Why?"

Y

Yes Pattern	Creating "Yes" responses by customers during your presentation so that the inclination to say "No" at the close is greatly diminished.

INDEX

INSURING CONTINUED SUCCESS...

Since learning is an ongoing experience, I encourage you to continue your quest for success by investing in yourself and your business. Here's how...

- Request our catalog of audio, CD and video programs designed to reinforce fundamentals and introduce innovative strategies that establish you as the recognized expert in your field. Make them an important piece to your business library.

- Inquire about my national and international public appearances, custom seminars and workshops, corporate presentations and ongoing training programs. My assistant will be happy to send you a schedule, additional information, or contact you in person to address your specific needs.

- Send your questions, observations, and personal accounts that occurred as a result of reading this book and adopting my principles on *Investigative Selling*. Who knows, perhaps you'll be a contributor to my next book.

OMAR PERIU

Omar Periu conducts sales training and motivational seminars nationally and internationally, specializing in:

- Sales Training
- Sales Management Training
- Motivational Seminars
- Conventions
- Audio, CD, Video Cassettes

If you want your next Meeting or Convention to be a guaranteed success and leave a lasting impression on your people, call or write for more information or a free product catalog:

Omar Periu International, Inc.
P.O. Box 812470
Boca Raton, FL 33481
(800) 789-3282 • (561) 479-2300 • Fax (561) 479-2282
e-mail: OPeriu@aol.com